THE FREEDOM OF
THE PREACHER

THE MACMILLAN COMPANY
NEW YORK · BOSTON · CHICAGO · DALLAS
ATLANTA · SAN FRANCISCO

MACMILLAN & CO., LIMITED
LONDON · BOMBAY · CALCUTTA
MELBOURNE

THE MACMILLAN CO. OF CANADA, LTD.
TORONTO

THE FREEDOM OF THE PREACHER

BY

WILLIAM PIERSON MERRILL
Minister of the Brick Presbyterian Church
in the City of New York

THE LYMAN BEECHER LECTURES ON
PREACHING, FOR THE YEAR 1922

New York
THE MACMILLAN COMPANY
1922

Press of
J. J. Little & Ives Company
New York, U. S. A.

"Life is freedom, inserting itself within necessity, and turning it to its profit."

HENRI BERGSON.

CONTENTS

I
THE PROPHET

THE FREEDOM
OF THE PREACHER

CHAPTER I

THE PROPHET

THE prophet is the preacher's ideal. The humblest preacher looks at the spokesman of God, afire with the truth, filled with the Spirit, accredited by the touch of the Eternal Word, and says, "That is what I would be, if I could." Yet few attain to the ideal.

The preacher is at once more and less than the prophet:—widely more, immeasurably less. More, because he must serve and run and walk on many lines, while the prophet sends his full fiery force down one straight line; less, because only at rare moments, if at all, does he enter into the glory of inspiration, when he knows that what he speaks is the living word of the living God to living men, which they question at their peril.

These lectures are designed for preachers, rather than for prophets, for the many who stand in common places, not for the few called to stand on some Mount Carmel. Yet, just because the prophet is the preacher's ideal, and because, few though they be, the prophets are the choicest possession of the church and among

1

the greatest gifts God bestows on the race, we may
well begin the discussion of freedom of speech in the
pulpit, its rights and limits, with a clear declaration
of the right and necessity of prophetic liberty.

The prophet means more to religion than any other
man, or all other men taken together. There is simply
no comparison between him and the priest, as to their
value to religion.

The church has leaped forward at those rare times
when prophets appeared, men speaking with authority,
and not as scribes. The church has languished or
moved at a dull, dead pace, when authority was all
found by scribes, in the past and its records. As one
reads church history, he wonders if the most typical
scene in it may not be that in which, after Judas Mac-
cabaeus had recaptured Jerusalem, the leaders of the
victorious Judeans debated what to do with the dese-
crated altar. Swine's flesh had been offered upon it.
It had become an unholy thing. How might it be
cleansed? Could it be cleansed at all? Unable to
decide aright, they carefully laid the stones of the altar
aside "until a prophet should arise, who should tell
them what the will of the Lord was." All through
the course of religious history, we see the wisest men,
the saintliest, the boldest, laying aside practical problems, great questions, until there should stand up a
man of God, a prophet, who would know what should
be done.

How the prophet is needed throughout the world's
life to-day! Never has there been so vivid and profound and diffused a consciousness that things are
wrong, so utter a bewilderment as to how they may
be set right. There is an excess of critical analysis,
and a dearth of constructive synthesis. We are tak-

ing down our altars, educational, political, physical, ecclesiastical, social; we are conscious that they have been defiled by the foulness of war; we are carefully setting the stones one side, until a prophet shall arise to tell us what the will of the Lord is. We long to hear his voice, but we do not detect it either crying in the wilderness or arresting the attention of the city's busy throng. Priests? We have enough of them, far too many. Ministers? They tell us there is a dearth of them, but we suspect that the truth is that the world wants fewer churches served by fewer and better men. But how we need a prophet or two, who can see straight and far, can speak with passion and with authority, and can prepare the way of the Lord, laying straight into the dim time to come the lines on which God's Kingdom may get forward.

It is not in religion only that the prophet is needed. Everywhere there is the call for men of imaginative insight, moral passion, and the voice of authority. Yet always there will be a certain spiritual aloofness, a definitely religious character, about the prophet. Very likely he will not be a churchman; but certainly he will not be a business man. It is eternally significant that the great hero who stands out from the mists of ancient history like a granite mountain half-seen through the fog, the man the impress of whose greatness is on all modern civilization, was neither priest nor ruler, but man of God. Moses made priests; he appointed rulers; but he was unquestionably above them all, though he held no office. And this man, the one indispensable man in the whole horde, was most at home in the "Tent of Meeting," where his soul was alone with God's spirit. One of the best promises in all the wealth of divine assurances of good is the promise that from time to time God will raise up a prophet like unto him. God's greatest gift, man's sorest need, is such a prophet.

Always, for such a prophet, the tent of meeting, or the meeting house, will be the real home. It is to the church, more than to any other institution of society, that we turn, and have a right to turn, for the leaders the world needs for its moral and spiritual guidance.

Two practical questions present themselves: What can we of the church do to facilitate the coming of the prophet? And, What shall we do with him when he appears?

What can the church do to stimulate and foster the production of prophets?

It is of the very essence of the prophetic gift that it cannot be standardized. It is not subject to the working of that process called "Quantity Production," best illustrated in the making of Ford cars. No mechanism will avail. The true prophet is hand-made, and the hand that makes him is that of the most High. There will always be few of them, under the most favorable conditions; and the moments when ordinary preachers, artists, statesmen, and editors catch a bit of the prophetic gleam, must be far between.

Yet we might and should have more of such men, and more of such moments, than we do. We would have more, if we prepared the way for them. It is well to remember how once four great seers came within a few years of each other. Something in the eighth century before Christ favored the emergence of the prophet. How can we reproduce those conditions? It is well also to remember the long centuries of barrenness and mechanism, when no voice was heard to speak with original authority. It would be well could we realize how, in every century, men who might have been spokesmen for God have dwindled into phonographs, playing standardized records. How many youths every year who might have spoken with prophetic power have had the spark of inspiration quenched by the untoward conditions in church and school and social order, God alone knows. Did we know it, we would be appalled at the criminal waste of the world's greatest treasure.

Our social life is, to far too great an extent, organized to quench inspiration and encourage conformity. It is quite inevitable that our state schools should be mainly devoted to the production of the largest possible number of average useful citizens, men and women so trained that we know how they will act in given conditions. That is one half of the problem of democratic training,—the more obvious, the simpler, immensely the larger part in bulk. But the other and more decisive half we are leaving to chance forces, the fostering of individuality, the production of leaders, whose conduct is not predictable under given conditions, because they look at conditions not as fixed arbiters of fate, but as plastic elements to be shaped to the service of ideals.

In an age of standardized education, when practical efficiency is the goal, and training becomes more and more vocational, and the individual withers in the process, the church should view it as one of its supreme aims to correct this false emphasis, and to encourage that development of soul which is fading out of our educational processes more and more.

How can the church do this?

First of all, by insisting on the adequate recognition, all through our educational processes, of the truth that religion is an indispensable element in education for citizenship; by using all the influence it possesses or can set in motion to make this recognition operative in the educational processes of America.

Every true American will guard with jealous care the established American policy of the separation of church and state. Better education utterly devoid of religion than education controlled by any one religious body, or used as a field for sectarian disputes and rivalries. It is very hard, it may be impossible, to make religion an integral part of the training in our state schools. Something vastly more is needed than the reading of the Bible, and it is hard to provide even that.

But there are private schools, colleges, and universities. They came forth from the life of the church. They are free, as state institutions cannot be, to follow whatever they see to be the true line of development in the training of youth. The church should exert all the influence it can wield to make such schools and colleges see their opportunity and duty to demonstrate the superiority of an education which makes generous provision for religious culture. Let the universities and colleges stand like a rock against any and every attempt to limit freedom of thought or to restrict the absolute rights of the scientific method and its results. The Church should heartily stand with the educational institutions in this, quick to resent and to resist the intrusion of ecclesiastical influence into the field of facts where science has absolute right to free operation. But the church should insist, and the universities and colleges should recognize, that religion is as important an element in true culture as is science, and that it should be given equal freedom and encouragement. No college would dream of leaving the cultivation of the sciences to a voluntary organization of the students. It is equally foolish to leave the cultivation of religion to a voluntary organization of the students. Just as a college feels it to be its duty to see that every member of its faculty shall possess the scientific spirit and attitude, and rightly judges that to make 〃 requirement is no infringement of the sacred p... ple of academic freedom, so should it demand ✓ that every member of the faculty shall possess the religious spirit and attitude, rightly understanding that such a demand does not in the least impair the proper working of the principle of academic freedom. It would be wrong to require that all members of the faculty of a college or any designated percentage of them, should be members of any particular religious body; but it is fair and right to require that no man or woman shall teach in any department, no matter how brilliant his intellect or how thorough his special equipment, who is not reverent and sympathetic in his attitude toward religion, and that for the simple and sufficient reason that religion is an essential element in the character and equipment of an American citizen.

Why cannot our great privately-endowed and privately-controlled universities and colleges and schools see that to them is given the opportunity—to them almost exclusively—to work out one of the hardest and most urgent of the problems in our national life, the problem of holding together knowledge and religion for the production of sound manhood and womanhood? When will some one of these great schools see and seize its opportunity to announce as its policy that the religious spirit and attitude shall henceforth be given

the same freedom and recognition as the scientific attitude and spirit, and for the same reason, a conviction
that it is necessary for sound training of youth? It
ought to be as impossible to choose as head of such an
institution a man who does not believe whole-heartedly
in God as it now is to choose a man who does not
believe whole-heartedly in the spirit and method of
modern science.

But inside its own life the church can do much to
foster the free spirit of prophecy.

2. For one thing, the church can consciously and inde-
fatigably stand for the culture and encouragement of
the personal life.

There is much talk about the dwindling function of
the church in the social order. Some tell us, with
sorrow, and some with satisfaction, but all with assurance of fact, that the church has been slowly but surely
crowded out and back until little part is left to it in the
real ongoing of life. Once education was in its hands,
the care of the sick, the administration of charity, the
cure of souls. Now the state educates, public and private philanthropy cares for the sick and poor, and the
psychoanalyst looks after the soul. Has the church
ceased to have a true *raison d'être?*

At the least, however, there is this one function of
immense and growing importance which the church
can discharge better than any other institution. It is
the function of fostering the personal life in a day of
mass movements, organized forces, and standardized
living. It is no small task to be the chief agent for
fortifying the soul against giving way to mechanism
and externalism.

If the church would "serve the present age," justify
its existence and its place in the social order, and

stimulate the possibilities of the prophetic in men and of the appearance of the prophet among men, let it resist to the utmost in its own life the tendency to trust in mass movement and organized effort and standardized machinery, and set itself to reminding men of the preëminence of the person, the sacredness of individuality, what our fathers called "the worth of the soul." Somehow every Sunday the ministry of the pulpit, and of the entire church service, should convey to men and women, benumbed, beaten down, lost in the crowd all the week, the message: "You are worth something in yourself, apart from the crowd, aside from your social relations. Let the thing that is hidden in your heart come out and sun itself here in the presence of God's Spirit."

In one of the letters of William James is a paragraph much quoted of late, which the church might well take as the statement of its spirit and attitude:—

"As for me, my bed is made: I am against bigness and greatness in all their forms, and with the invisible molecular forces that work from individual to individual, stealing in through the crannies of the world like so many soft rootlets, or like the capillary oozing of water, and yet rending the hardest monuments of man's pride if you give them time. The bigger the unit you deal with, the hollower, the more brutal, the more mendacious is the life displayed. So I am against all the big organizations as such, national ones first and foremost; and in favor of the eternal forces of truth which always work in the individual and immediately unsuccessful way—underdogs always, till history comes, after they are long dead, and puts them on the top."

To adopt, and steadfastly to maintain that attitude, would be to encourage the prophet and the prophetic.

There is acute and severe arraignment of the thoughts
and ways of to-day in the saying of Gerald Stanley
Lee: "Some people wonder how Jesus of Nazareth
ever accomplished anything, when He never was a
member of a Committee." Ministers are too readily
content with a church that is a huge machine for good
works, with every member properly geared into it.
The weekly bulletin of a prominent church proudly
proclaims: "In *this* church even the babies are organized." We must come back to the realization that the
church is here for the intensive cultivation of personality. And only to such a church, that takes that as
its chief end and aim, perpetually calling men to be
souls and not cogs, will the messenger of the covenant
ever appear. Out of such a church will come men to
speak with authority in the name of the Lord, men in
whose hearts the spark of inspiration would have been
speedily quenched in youth, had not the house of God
cared for it, feeding and fanning it week by week, year
after year.

Every preacher should go into his pulpit every Sunday full of faith in the absolute and unquestionable
preëminence of the spiritual; fearful lest the divine
flame of the prophetic gift should be quenched in some
child or youth there present; in a very agony of dread
lest, through dullness or insensitiveness on his own
part, he thicken rather than keep plastic the cooling
and hardening surface of the souls before him. "Thirty
minutes to raise the dead" is Ruskin's definition of a
sermon. Can any one ask a heavier responsibility, a
more important function, than that? Let the church
service first of all and all through be alive and life-
giving, calling out and encouraging the personal life,
the play of individuality, the flame of the spirit.

Josiah Royce was not far from the inmost truth of the matter when he said that the great saying: "This mortal must put on immortality" meant that this general and common human nature must "take on individuality." That should be the high calling of every sermon and every prayer and every song, not only to the end of reviving the dying flame of personality in the souls of all, but also for the glorious chance that some time in the atmosphere of such thought and feeling one of God's great spokesmen may be caught, roused from growing lethargy, and started on the way to be a prophet among men. It would be sufficient to justify the existence of the American church, the time and strength and resources spent in its maintenance, if somewhere in this land, sometime within the next decade, the divine flame in the soul of a single youth were, through the influence of the church, kept from dying, fanned and fed until it became a fire in the bones, and an Isaiah, an Amos, or a Jeremiah appeared in our national life. One such prophetic figure would be worth infinitely more than the cost of the church. And part of the glory of preaching is that one never knows whether the ministry of his own pulpit may not be the humble but effectual means of saving a true man of God from death of the spirit, and leading him into the exercise of the prophetic function.

If we would increase the prophetic element in the life of our time, we must also care for our church schools, and for the religious education of our youth. A great many earnest and able men and women are awake to the importance of religious education, and are doing valiant service in its cause; but too often they put all their efforts into making church schools more pedagogically perfect; and pedagogical perfection may stifle rather than stimulate the prophetic impulse. One could scarcely find a surer way to kill, as by a late frost, the buds of prophecy in a child's soul than by intrusting his spiritual nurture to a church school the chief aim of which was accuracy of pedagogical method. The aim of all our religious education should be inspiration, the kindling of the imagination, the deepening of the God-instinct, the confirming in strength and steadiness of every impulse of worship, service, and devotion, the setting free of the soul. Right method can help wonderfully in that task; and we should welcome and use all that educationists can tell us as to ways and means; let nothing that I am saying be used as a plea against the fullest advance in educational method on the part of all our church schools. But let method be servant, not master; means, not end. Better far intrust a growing child to a teacher or class-leader who is fervent in spirit but wrong in method, than to one who is correct in method but cold in heart; better the teacher who is ignorant of pedagogical method and hopeless in theological outlook, but whose sense of reality is vivid and wholesome, whose faith in Christ is a living passion, who will surround the child's soul with the holy influences of prayer and belief, and will continually call that soul to the worship and following of eternal ideals, than the teacher smoothly correct in every detail of instruction, and faultlessly equipped with the most modern view of things, but caring more for the mind's hold on facts than for the soul's hold on God. The best hope that our church schools shall prove to be, in the truest sense, schools of the prophets, where no divine spark shall be quenched, but all shall be quickened, lies in the presence and power, through all their teachers and leaders, of a passionate faith in the ideal and eternal possibilities of youth, an eager and prayerful determination to bring to full consciousness and free development the sacred grace of personality in every child, and to lead it to the altar as a whole burnt-offering.

The church can do something to encourage the production of prophets by emphasizing the importance of home life and of home training in religion.

Here is the most vital and indispensable source of the prophetic in our social life. Men of God come out of godly homes. Moses, Samuel, John the Baptist, Jesus,—their biographers do not feel that they have adequately accounted for the line these great souls took and followed until they have told us of their birth, yes, of the longings and prayers, the faith and devotion, of their parents before their birth. Prophets are made by their fathers and mothers more than by any other human influences. Out of homes where God is known come the men that know Him; they know Him so well because, from earliest days, they have lived with Him every day.

If the church would provide prophets in the day of the world's deep need of guidance, let the church do its utmost to revive and deepen and broaden family religion; let it seek to inspire parents with a vision of what their sons and daughters may be if they take in the consciousness of God with their daily food, and breathe His spirit in the atmosphere of the home, and receive His great ideals as a simple heritage. Even were the priests as weak as Eli, or as wicked as his sons, and even were the ark of God in the hands of the enemy, there would still arise men like Samuel, were there mothers like Hannah; yes, men like Jesus, were there mothers like Mary. It is not easy to see or to say just how the church may best exert real influence over the home life; but certainly the church is better able to exert such influence than is any other factor in our social order. And what would count for more in our common life than the exerting by the church of a strong and steady influence over parents, making them see the power and glory which they may bring to light if they will set their children in the way of God's thoughts and purposes.

The church can do much to encourage the growth of the prophetic spirit by giving larger freedom in its own ongoing for the play of individuality in religion. There is a strong conviction, and it is too fully justified by facts, that the church prizes conformity rather than freedom, and likes the old better than the new; that it holds back the makers of trails and honors those who drive in the ruts. So far as this is true the church is discouraging the prophets and making their appearance less probable.

The church ought to be known as the institution which, more than any other, calls men and incites them to freedom, freedom of thought, of speech, of action. Were that the common and current impression of the spirit and attitude of the church, we should see some of the finest and most promising of our youth eagerly entering the ministry, which now they pass by with scarcely a thought that it may be the place for them. Once let the church begin to put a premium on boldness and the ministry will become the most honored and sought of the professions.

Prophets are born, not made. Yet birth is not enough; newborn babes may be killed or stunted or developed to the fulfillment of their promise, according to the way they are treated. Once let all our theological schools begin to watch for the germs of prophetic power, to welcome freedom rather than conformity, to look on their students as possible dynamos rather than as possible storage-plants, and these schools of the prophets may become producers of prophetic leaders of the life of the world.

But the church at large must also play its part in maintaining that atmosphere of freedom in which alone prophets naturally grow. When shall we see sessions and presbyteries, standing committees and councils of ordination, churches and congregations, in their choice of men for the ministry caring more for freedom of spirit than for conformity, delighted at every revelation of original thought and feeling, more afraid of quenching the spirit and despising prophesyings than of allowing variations from the faith once delivered by the doctors? Once there was a youth who sat in the midst of the theological leaders of His day and of His church, asking them questions, and astonishing them with the freedom and originality of his point of view, and He became the preacher Who "spake as never man spake." Once two men stood before an ecclesiastical council and were recognized as companions of Jesus by their *boldness*. The same characteristic might put them on probation or under suspicion in many an ecclesiastical council to-day. What an age of glory and power would dawn for the church if ecclesiastical bodies, great and small, should prize above all evidences of conformity and correctness that freedom wherewith Christ hath made us free, and should find surest proof of the presence and guidance of the Holy Spirit in that liberty of soul which is always found where the Spirit of the Lord is. One of

the grave and persistent sins of the church through all
the ages has been reluctance to trust the leading of
the Holy Spirit unless He leads us along well-trodden
paths. Under such conditions, prophets must fight
their way, and many of them fall by the way. It is
well to stand for "soundness in the faith;" but we may
at least remember that it is the "aged men" who are
exhorted to be "sound in the faith," and that they are
also urged to be equally sound in love and in patience,
qualities they do not always display in dealing with
their younger brethren. One of the grave matters for
which the church must give account in the Day of
Judgment is the choking of prophetic promise in ecclesiastical examinations, or in hidebound churches
and church commissions, where those who might have
been voices of the Lord have been dulled into echoes
of ecclesiastical councils.

What shall we do with the prophet when he comes?
Two things! [1] First of all we must give him an unlimited allotment of freedom. We must clear the track
and let him run at full speed.

Freedom is not only the necessary condition of his
appearance, it is the necessary atmosphere of his con-
tinuing power and influence. The church will never
have very many prophets; let it try severely and thoroughly all who aspire to that office; but once the
church finds a man in whom is anything of the fire of
prophecy, let its policy be that enunciated by the tomb
of Lazarus, "Loose him and let him go."

This is the first thing, to leave the prophet free,
absolutely untrammeled! [2] The second thing is to follow him, to trust his prophetic leading.

The lament of the Eternal Wisdom over every age
and stage in the religious development of humanity

might well be, "O fools, and slow of heart to believe
all that the prophets have spoken." It is only half
to leave the prophet free. If he goes on alone and we
stay in our tents or in our burrows, he fails and we
fail.

A certain measure of opposition, of hard fighting,
may be necessary to the making of the prophet. But
once he has proved himself, what would it not mean
if the church took up its baggage and followed him,
or even followed, leaving its impedimenta behind!
Sometimes we wonder what the church would be now,
what the world would be, had Israel whole-heartedly
followed Amos or Isaiah, had the church as a whole
followed Savonarola or Wiclif or Luther. What would
the American Episcopal Church be now, had it followed with all its heart Phillips Brooks? The tragic
fact is that we have let the prophets go forward alone,
or have followed in their train afar off, timidly, and by
compulsion of outward, slow-moving circumstance.

Of course the plea for prophetic freedom and for
implicit following when the prophet appears does not
mean that we should accept every self-commissioned
representative of the Lord. We must try the spirits,
for many a man stands up and claims to be a prophet
who is only an egotist. We need to face many would-
be leaders of religious progress with a question the
shrewd Scotch mother put to her son after she had
heard him preach a woeful sermon and then heard him
protest that God had called him to be a preacher,
"Jock, lad, are ye sure it was no some other noise that
ye heard?"

But it is not impossible to identify the true voice
of prophecy with clear certainty. This we may know
always, that personal pretensions and forward-thrust-

ings of self are utterly inconsistent with the character
of a true man of God. The man who insists on being
regarded as a prophet may instantly be written down
as mistaken. Fundamental to the character of every
true spokesman of God, every leader of the spiritual
advance of humanity, is a great and deep <u>humility</u>
which would keep him silent and lost in the crowd but
for the overwhelming compulsion of a message which
must be spoken. Every prophet bears that hall-mark
of humility. Moses shrinks from the task: "Who am
I? I am not eloquent, either before or since Thou
hast spoken to Thy servant." Amos disclaims any
prophetic authority: "I am not a prophet, nor the son
of a prophet. I am a herdsman. But the Lord Jehovah
hath spoken; who can but prophesy?" Isaiah cries out
of an unclean heart and unclean lips. Jeremiah pro-
tests that he is a child, utterly incapable of great words
or works. John the Baptist disclaims the very titles
Christ later gives him. He is no Elijah, no prophet;
he is just a voice. So the true prophet always comes,
asking no recognition for himself, accredited only by
the obvious and unassailable truth of his message,
eager to be but a voice for the message of the Living
Spirit of the Eternal. Give all men the right to speak
freely; encourage liberty of prophesying to the fullest
extent; loose the bands of ecclesiastical conformity;
and then follow with heart and soul and mind and
strength those leaders, and those only, whose words
bear the stamp of their origin in the spirit of the Living God, revealed in Christ our Lord, sealed with the
grace of a deep, true, humbleness of spirit.

Freedom is the atmosphere in which the prophetic
spirit may thrive; freedom for the prophet when he
appears, that no syllable of the Word from God

through him may be lost to us and to the world through repression; freedom and promptitude in following him, however strange the path he takes; that is a condition of true Christian progress. The church of to-day should hold every other consideration secondary to the recovery of the fire of the Spirit, that once more God may lead His church and His world through His chosen and inspired messengers.

> This, this is he for whom the world is waiting,
> To sing the beatings of its mighty heart.

God send the prophets; and God grant us grace to know them when they come, to give them free course, and to follow them whithersoever they may lead.

II
THE PREACHER

CHAPTER II

THE PREACHER

If all the Lord's preachers were prophets, the matter of their freedom would be easy in theory, however difficult it might remain in practice. For the right way would simply be to let them have free course and be glorified. The prophet is like the special train, for which everything else must be side switched, while it thunders down the main line, the track cleared for its swift and unimpeded passage.

But there are few special trains, and many regular expresses, locals, and freights, making their way over the line. There must be much adapting of individual preference to general necessity, much obedience to orders, a great deal of accommodation. The question of freedom becomes an important and an intricate one, when we deal with the ordinary train or the average preacher.

What are the "metes and bounds of liberty" in the case of the average preacher? How shall he achieve the largest possible measure of freedom consistent with the best possible service in his church and community?

There is a wide difference of judgment as to the opportunity for freedom in the life of the average minister. Some will tell us that the minister is, of all men in the community, the one most hampered by conventional restrictions, least free to live his own life and go his own way, most bound by precedent and custom.

Others will declare the minister to be the freest man in the community. Where does the truth lie between those two extremes?

Let this be said first of all: The ministry, like all other professions, has certain natural obligations and restrictions which it lays upon the man who enters it. And he is acting in an unjustifiable and foolish manner who, entering it, chafes at the entirely normal restrictions which it demands. The freedom which the right-minded minister seeks is, above all, freedom to be a good minister, not freedom from the natural and rightful obligations and limitations of his calling. No man should stay in any calling who is not cheerfully willing to pay the full price of remaining therein.

We may well set as our motto in dealing with the question of the freedom of the preacher the great definition of LIFE given by Henri Bergson:—"Life is freedom, inserting itself within necessity, turning it to its profit." That is the minister's life. He enters a network of necessity, fixed ways, customs, precedents. If it only serves to entangle him, so that he cannot move readily, to bind him and hold him down, he will be made ineffective by it, and will fail in his work. But he will be certain to fail at least as completely if he tears the net, breaks the bonds, and tramps on his rough-shod way. His free soul must insert itself within the necessity, and, keeping itself free, turn the necessity to its profit; not defying the conventional, but making it serve the spiritual; not flying in the face of established custom, but out of its heavier-than-air material forming a machine that will lift him with itself and fly like an eagle. It is one of the fundamental problems of the life and work of the minister, how far he may be free, how far he must be bound; what limits he must respect; how his freedom may realize itself within the bounds of necessity, and work out therein the glory of God.

We shall touch specifically on certain outstanding phases of this problem in the next five lectures. In this one we think of the general problem, especially as related to the personal life and conduct of the minister, and his preparation for pulpit ministry. I know I shall be pardoned if there sounds from the discussion far more of the note of personal experience than is usually comfortable for a speaker or acceptable for his hearers.

The man who enters the ministry finds himself, as do men in few other callings, fitted with habits of a conventional cut. The clerical garb is a symbol of something strongly operative even in the lives of those who eschew the wearing of it. There is a more or less widely accepted ideal of what the minister should do and should not do, how he should dress and act; there are certain presuppositions as to his habits and customs. We may well be glad that there is far less of this artificial idea in operation than in times gone by. There are few communities now in which the minister is compelled to restrain his sense of humor on pain of being adjudged "worldly." It is only on the stage or in comic weeklies that the minister is still understood to be a sanctimonious, silly, fussy, effeminate creature, shocked at strong language, quite at home at pink teas, set apart from a manly life. But there remains, in many a parish, a sort of mental and spiritual uniform ready for the minister to don.

This is the place for a cheerful assertion of free individuality. It is a much mooted question whether a minister should or should not indulge in certain practices commonly used with entire freedom by respectable men and women in the membership of the church. Should he attend the theater, play cards, use tobacco, and the like? "Trivial questions," we say impatiently; but sometimes they are not too trivial to wreck a man's usefulness if he make a misstep in the direction of one of them. Should he or should he not adopt distinctive dress or other professional mark? He should face all such questions seriously and with the exercise of the best thought and judgment of which he is capable. But this is perfectly clear,—that the man who abstains from this or adopts that custom simply because the conventional idea of a minister in the particular community includes that particular action, is wrong, wholly wrong, only wrong. Freedom should be accommodating and ready to sacrifice; but it should never abdicate.

Is not one of the chief duties of the minister to sharpen the faculty of moral discrimination in his people? To that end he must draw definite lines always between those things which are to be classified as right and wrong because of their clearly marked social value or harmfulness, and those things which are called right and wrong only because people have agreed to call them so. Here example will speak far louder than precept.

A minister ought to have and to show great consideration for those commonly called weak brethren,—a somewhat incongruous designation for some of them, in view of the bulldog tenacity with which they cling to their opinions and judgments. But he ought also to have a care, in the sight of God, lest through undue yielding he confirm them in their narrow prejudices. It is one thing to be patient and considerate of the weak; it is quite another thing,—and a disastrous thing it is,—to be bullied by the weak. Conformity to their prejudices will leave them weaker. There are congregations which need nothing so much as a clean blast of moral reality such as would come from the presence of a minister who, in habits and ways of personal conduct, should walk straight through their prejudices with sturdy stride and cheerful mien.

This is the principle—is it not?—which may well guide in relation to these little, but vexing and often important, questions of personal action and conduct,— that the preacher shall do that, and that only, which commends itself to his own free conscience and judgment in the sight of God, as likely to make him a better man among his fellows and a better minister in his church and in the community?

We have a right contempt for the minister who abstains from certain common practices solely for the reason that it is expected of him as a minister, in deference to mere blind tradition, that he shall so abstain. But we ought to have a contempt even stronger for the minister who indulges in such practices simply because he intends to assert his personal liberty, whatever any one may think, or whatever the effect may be on other minds and lives. The man in the ministry who will not hold each and every matter of personal freedom subordinate to the consideration of the largest possible influence for Christ in the community is not worth his salt. How can he talk to any one about readiness to sacrifice?

Here then, as elsewhere, a man needs all his wisdom, all his poise, all his consecrated sense of divine guidance, that he may neither wound sensitive consciences nor confirm unreasonable prejudices; that he may neither exalt petty personal indulgences into obstinate and inflexible principles, nor fail to strike for the right of the Christian to be free from those "empty ways of living handed down from our fathers," from which St. Peter tells us that Christ died to set men free. The minister must seek in all his personal living to be a faithful example of the proper interplay of freedom and love.

He may well remind himself at times that he is by his very profession brought into peculiarly intimate relations with people and that therefore manners make the man far more than is true in other professions. To be slovenly in dress, or careless in personal habits, to fail in courtesy or graciousness, is a serious matter for a minister. One of the best known teachers of candidates for the ministry a score of years ago used to tell his pupils that "there are two invariable rules for success in the ministry, namely, 'pray without ceasing, and shave every morning.'"

Every preacher rightly aspires to be a free man in the preparation and delivery of his message. No bondage is more distasteful than slavery in the process of self-expression. *must have system*

Yet here the average preacher needs great good sense and discrimination, that he may clearly discern wherein true freedom consists, and how it may best be attained. The fact that Henry Ward Beecher found his sermons for Sunday evenings as he walked in his garden for a few minutes Sunday afternoons proves not that that is the ideal method, nor that all men would find their way to true freedom of expression by following his example, but only that he was a rarely gifted soul. I have known men who, seeking to be free by following Mr. Beecher's method, have simply succeeded in becoming slaves to their own slovenliness. Here, as always, the prophet is a law to himself, and an inspiration and a challenge to others rather than an example, a leader of the spirit rather than a teacher of method.

In truth, every man must make his own way into that freedom of utterance which is the goal sought by every public speaker. And he must be sure that he seeks and finds the best rather than the easiest way. There is only one ultimate test of methods, "by their fruits ye shall know them."

This is sure for most of us,—that the largest and most satisfactory freedom we can attain will come through strict discipline. In the production of any work of art, a strange and delicate adjustment is necessary between inspiration and diligence. It is a foolish saying that genius is only the infinite capacity for taking pains. Were that true, every German would be a genius, and every ant-hill would be an art gallery. But it is true, deeply and eternally true, that genius gets nowhere without unlimited willingness to take pains. Ruskin defines an artist as "one who has submitted to a law which it was painful to obey, in order that he may bestow a delight which it is gracious to bestow." That is the plain path for most preachers. In their patience they win their souls. There is a freedom about Fritz Kreisler's playing that cannot be approached by an æolian harp. Here and there appears a divinely gifted soul which seems to do the right thing by instinct. Yet, even in such cases, we are surprised, as we come to closer contact, at plain evidence of hard work, of resolute and steadfast discipline. Few works of art are more surely stamped as products of genuine and perfect inspiration than is the Andante movement from Beethoven's "Fifth Symphony." We are struck by its charming artlessness. But it happens that the notebook has been preserved in which was jotted down the theme as it first occurred to the composer, and the changes subsequently made in it. It is a commonplace theme; one's first reaction is that almost any one of average talent and a simple knowledge of music might have written out that bit. Then one follows along through the changes which, after months of reflection and patient care, produced the exquisite melody and harmonic setting recognized by all as worthy of immortality. We call it artless, but it is the result of the patient application of consummate art. As completed, it is far more free than in its original form. It was the patient, persistent work of the artist which wrought the freedom. There are a few glorious bits of music, like some of Schubert's creations, which joyously affirm: "I was free-born"; but most of the mighty masterpieces of art soberly declare: "With a great price obtained I this freedom."

Among modern masters of musical composition there are few who make so strong an impression of absolute spontaneity, passion, and inspiration, as does Tschaikowsky. You imagine his music as surging, white-hot, from his soul in some exalted mood. Yet it is precisely Tschaikowsky, of all the modern masters of music, who has left on record the rigid discipline out of which his art took shape. Every day, he tells us in his memoirs, he went to his desk and wrote music. Much of it was trash, finding a speedy end in the waste basket. All his good music, he says, was the product of exalted and special moods. But he was convinced not only that that daily rigid routine, writing whether or no he felt like doing it, facilitated the

full use of the mood when it came, but that often it
led to moments of inspiration which would never have
come without the steady attention to the practice of
the art to which he held himself with inflexible resolution.

One of the greatest temptations to which the
preacher is subject is to use his liberty as an occasion
to the flesh. There are few vocations in which a man
is so free to choose his own method, to make his own
schedule of work, to keep training or to break it, as in
the ministry. The average preacher, wanting to follow the gleam, must eternally beware lest he follow a
will-o'-the-wisp of irresponsible freedom into a swamp
of ill-prepared and slovenly talk. The wise minister
will begin with a schedule of regular work for the
week, an assignment of hours to which he will—not
rigidly, but very faithfully—adhere, even at considerable cost. Such a method will mean, of course, that
sometimes a sermon will be dragged out painfully,
word by word, in a dreary and wearisome process, on a
day wholly devoid of inspiration. But in the long run
sermons produced from a life that is faithful in self-
discipline, a life that works conscientiously according
to a well-designed schedule, will average far higher
in value than sermons produced by the man who waits
for the mood, and then writes in a fury. I have known
a considerable number of preachers who scorned sched-
ules, and waited for the proper moods, because they
would be free. And in every case the result has been
not a growing liberty, but an increasing tendency to
put off sermon-preparation to Saturday, which became
thereby a day of slavish torment, full of discomfort for
themselves and for their households. Instead of following the divine example, working for six days and

resting on the seventh, they trifle through the week
and spend the seventh day in frantic and nervous toil.
And this is true in almost every case, that the preachers
within the range of my knowledge who have thus
waited for moods have grown less effective with the
passing of the years, while those who have worked
faithfully by prearranged schedule have become more
free and more effective with the advance of time.
Their thoughts have widened with the process of the
suns.

The false notion that lawlessness is more godlike
than law has worked havoc in more fields than the
theological. The idea that freedom is incompatible
with discipline has wrecked many a promising career
in the pulpit. In an application quite different from
the original, it is true that "eternal vigilance is the
price of liberty"; and that preacher is wise who will
ceaselessly watch and work and keep training, to the
end that he may be more free as the mouthpiece of
the Divine Spirit. Blessed is that man whose delight
is in the law, rather than in the lawlessness, of the
Lord.

Of course the preacher must always remember that
a schedule needs constant watching, lest it become a
tyrant. Only less foolish than the man who will not
submit to discipline is the man who forms a schedule
and then makes of it an unchangeable fetish. The
end, after all, is not the schedule, but the sermon.

It is the part of wisdom, as a man grows and
changes, to change his method of sermon-preparation
and delivery from time to time, and that radically. I
recall an interesting case of a man who did this with
good result. He went to a leader in the church and
asked for assistance in finding a new field. He said

that he had been ten years in one field, and he felt that
the people were so accustomed to him, his ways and
his words, that a change would be beneficial for him
and for the congregation. But no other field seemed
to open for him; and so, some months later, he came
again to his friend, and said, "I cannot get a new field,
but I am going to give my people a new minister."
He changed his methods in most radical fashion, in
preaching and pastoral work. He had been writing
and reading his sermons; he began to speak without
notes. Wherever he could find any other way of doing
anything that seemed as good as the way he had been
following, he changed and took the new way. The
result was new life all through the worship and service
of his church, and new satisfaction and joy for himself in his relationship with the church and its people.

It was my good fortune to be minister in one field
for nearly seventeen years. About midway in that
ministry, I deliberately made a radical change in my
method of pulpit-preparation. I believe the new
method was better adapted to my stage of development than the old; but even had it been in itself no
better, the change would have been wise, for the fresh-
ening of interest it brought to preacher and hearers.
Recently, under the stress of a sudden necessity, I have
made, with some foreboding, another radical change
in the method of preparing sermons. Again the results give decisive evidence of the wisdom of making
the change.

The preacher must make his way toward freedom
in the pulpit clearly and surely in three arts,—the art
of gathering material, the art of clear and ordered
thinking, and the art of effective delivery.

The minister who would be free can never avoid the

obligation to read and acquire material. He must read widely and insatiably. He should especially seek out books of human interest. Theological writings will be indispensable; but detective stories will have a value also. I suppose it is important that a minister should keep up with the progress of theology and church history and the other specialties of his profession. But I know it is vital, that he read much of good literature, of biography, fiction, poetry, history, all that in which the soul of man finds free expression, even though it has little or nothing of a distinctively religious flavor about it. He must not only study the Bible critically, that he may know its contents; he must read it appreciatively and uncritically, that he may catch its unrivaled style, and be caught in the swing of its mighty emotions. A good English style is as essential to the preacher as a good delivery wagon is to the grocer. There are too many men in the pulpit who know a good deal, and think well enough, but have never gained the mastery of effective and simple language, through much companionship with the best writers, through deliberate and painstaking cultivation of a homely forceful use of words. A preacher without skill in words is like a knight with no knowledge of sword play.

No less vital is the art of ordered thinking. In the long run men will be most impressed and most helped by sermons which, without making the logical framework stand out, nevertheless do proceed through ordered argument to a clearly indicated conclusion. There is too much preaching of the type described by a critic as "truly apostolic," because the preacher took a text and then, like the apostles, "went everywhere preaching the Gospel."

Among all the brilliant and forceful characteristics of the preaching of Horace Bushnell none is more significant than his daring fashion of announcing his theme at the outset, usually in the form of a thesis to be maintained. At once that method challenges attention, and compels the speaker to the discipline of ordered thinking. It may be overdone. Bushnell overdid it, with the result that his sermons at times have a scholastic flavor. But most of us would gain immensely from a habit of stating our subject in clear words, at least to ourselves, at the outset, and then carrying it through an ordered process of thought to an irresistible conclusion.

The subject, I say; yet we need to bear in mind that in preaching the object is even more important than the subject. Every sermon aims at definite action. It is meant to make a difference in the lives of the hearers, or it is no true sermon. Here also there is need of skill in orderly treatment, human as well as logical skill, that the object may be enforced at the end with full and compelling effect.

Because of the vital need of such ordered thinking, every preacher should from the beginning of his work subject himself to the discipline of thinking through his material. Especially should those gifted with fluency of utterance compel themselves to write and analyze. Most men can safely venture to preach by an ex tempore method only after years of careful practice in ordered thinking and writing.

In the preparation of sermons the wise preacher will avail himself of true labor-saving devices wherever possible; and that for two reasons: first, for the saving of his time for the details of modern pastoral work; and second, for the reaction upon his thought and style, that he may catch his thoughts as nearly as possible in fluid or living form. Thoughts harden with appalling rapidity; and he is fortunate and free who, through knowledge of stenography or abbreviated longhand, typewriting, or the use of dictation, can shorten the time of composition without impairing its quality, or even with addition to its value.

Of importance also to the real freedom of the preacher is careful attention to the art of delivery. There is vastly more involved in this than the externals of voice, gesture, and manner, but these are vital. There are few ministers who would not gain by instruction and practice in the art of delivery; and there are many who fail of the effect they might have, through lack of attention to the manner in which they present their message. Every preacher should be humble and eager in welcoming criticisms. I shall always thank God for what I gained once from that much-despised source, an anonymous letter.

But the chief concern in the delivery of the message is the condition of the man at the time of speaking. The preacher should give careful and constant attention to the problem of being at his best when in the pulpit. There are three main elements in the complete make-up of a good and effective sermon; the getting of a good subject; the working out of the material; and the state of mind and body and soul at the time of delivery. I would arrange these three in order of importance thus: first, the subject; second, the right condition of the speaker; and third, the work done in preparation. Experience and observation confirm that judgment more and more. It is hard or impossible to overestimate the importance of the physical and spiritual condition of the preacher at the time of the delivery of his message. Happy is the man who comes to the pulpit with a clear head, a clean heart, an unflurried mind, a confident faith, a sense of thorough well-being and vigor, and straight from personal contacts of an inspiring and not of a depressing sort. It is needless to say that of all personal contacts the best with which to preface preaching is calm and trustful prayer. I once had an elder, a good and useful man, whom I had to request particularly not to speak to me before the service. He left me blue and depressed. I know also what it means when the right sort of friends come for prayer with a minister before he goes into the pulpit.

One may easily fail to appreciate how much it means to the average busy man or woman to find in the pulpit Sunday morning a man obviously radiant with physical and spiritual energy. Recently a minister of my acquaintance was urged to undertake the conduct of a discussion class just before the morning worship. He received a very earnest note of protest from one of the most active and intelligent men in the congregation, begging him not to do it. "You do not know," he wrote, "the tremendous value to busy and tired men of contact with your fresh, vigorous, untired personality. The greatest service you render me is in that impression of spiritual vigor you give me each Sunday."

So, throughout his life and work, the preacher will best attain his high ideal and discharge his divine function, if he fulfils the conception of Bergson, of freedom inserting itself within necessity, and turning it to its profit. He will be happiest and most helpful who best realizes his freedom through happy adjustment to circumstance, that he may learn to become through the use of it a bigger and freer man. All around the average preacher are conventions, customs, obligations, demands, a network of necessity. It is futile and wasteful to rebel at it all, and insist upon a freedom that means the unrestrained exercise of one's present unrestrained self. It is pathetic to lose one's freedom in the tangle and go through the motions of the preacher, with never a flash of free inspiration, never free from the compulsion of the network of conventional influences. But it is glorious, a growing gain, a deepening joy, to maintain one's freedom within the network of necessity, actually becoming more free through increasing discovery of the way to turn necessity to the profit of one's work and the realization of one's ideals, entering more and more under the guidance of God's good Spirit of growth, into that larger, finer, more real freedom which comes only through full and glad submission to discipline, until necessity becomes simply the opportunity for a wider exercise of that liberty which is life.

CHAPTER III

THE PRIEST

THE sermon does not stand or fall alone. It is set in the midst of an ordered service of worship, more or less elaborate. The effect of the sermon may depend very largely upon the skill and insight with which sermon and service are made to function harmoniously and to a single end, so that a unified impression comes to the devout worshiper.

To some preachers the fact that the sermon is thus inextricably related to the other parts of public worship seems a restriction to be endured rather than welcomed. I have known preachers whose conduct during the opening part of the worship gave plain evidence that they were waiting, with none too great patience, for the coming of their real opportunity with the beginning of the sermon. They would view as the ideal situation such a condition as that which obtained at the City Temple in London in the old days, when Joseph Parker preached, and no one cared about any other detail. Or they wish the sermon could be like one of Joseph Cook's lectures, a *Ding an sich,* unrelated to other exercises.

In fact, however, the preacher has in the details of worship amid which his sermon is set a wonderful asset. If he is willing to restrict slightly his unlicensed freedom, and patiently plan to give to prayer and praise full scope, he will find these elements of worship giving wings to his words; greater power and greater freedom will come to his preaching for thoughtful and eager use of the values that lie in liturgy and music. Dr. Gunsaulus achieved a success in the Central Church of Chicago fairly comparable with that of Joseph Parker in London. And those who studied his methods know how largely that success was due to the care he gave to the worship, even making it a rule to attend the weekly rehearsal of his choir, and to give much time to counseling with the director of music, planning with him the details of every service.

There are parts of the worship for which the minister is no less directly responsible than for the sermon. These are the lessons from the Scriptures, the Responsive Readings, the prayers and the hymns.

Constant service in the pulpit has afforded me scant opportunity for observing the conduct of worship; but it is my decided conviction, based on such observation as I have been able to exercise, that, in our free or non-liturgical churches, there is a marked tendency to slight the value of these parts of the worship. There is often to be noted evidence of hasty selection and thoughtless rendering of the lessons from the Scriptures, of scant care in the choice of hymns, and of prayer unregulated as to length and order.

Here again we come upon a phase of the general struggle between freedom and order, where, as in other parts of it, the ideal course is neither slavery to order nor unlicensed liberty, but "freedom, inserting itself within necessity, and turning it to its profit." It seems beyond question that there are immense values in the free ideals and practice of our non-liturgical churches. There are more people who will respond to such worship than to a highly-regulated order, taking only our normal Protestant constituency into the account. And I am confident also that this tendency to find greater satisfaction in free than in prescribed worship will increase rather than diminish in the immediate future. Men are most moved by prayers that come from the heart at the time, and by readings from the Bible selected to voice the emotions and thoughts natural to the mental and spiritual state in which they find themselves on a particular Sunday.

But the minister to whom free prayer means thoughtless and irresponsible praying, and free selection of lessons hasty and careless selection, is abusing a great and sacred privilege, and wasting an immense advantage. Any one who sees in the practice of free prayer and free selection of lessons from the Scriptures only a matter of liberty has not begun to appreciate the meaning of it. It means the assumption of a heavier responsibility. Those who serve in liturgical churches possess a certain liberty which others lack. To attain real freedom, and to make full use of it as an agent in soul-culture, the minister in a non-liturgical church must give serious and costly attention to the conduct of public worship, the selection of readings, the choice of hymns, and the preparation of prayers, lest these, which the Westminster Directory for Worship rightly calls "the more important duties of prayer and praise," become mere adjuncts to the sermon. Better the most slavish use of prayer-book and rubric than the sort of freedom that exposes a congregation to the momentary whims of a careless soul. Here, as everywhere, freedom is a hardly won grace, a delicate adjustment to be worked out continually, an art to be acquired only by process of discipline.

No preacher is rendering what is due to himself, to

his congregation, to the Word of God, or to the church as a whole, who does not spend time and patient thought on the selection and preparation of the lessons to be read. Let me here avow myself a firm believer in the idea,—which it is the fashion to disparage just now,—the idea of unity of thought and spirit through an entire service, from beginning to end. I do not mean that hymns and prayers and all else shall be stretched into palpable and artificial uniformity, so that the service is like a harp with one string, the opening prayer clearly stating what the subject of the sermon is to be, and the closing prayer asking God's help to realize in our lives, one, two, three, as set forth in the sermon. That is a caricature of unity. There are weighty interests and common values, which should have first place always in the worship, whatever the subject of the sermon. But I do mean that, like a tinge of color, like a delicate but decided flavor, like a keynote dominating a rich harmony, some one great simple thought or spiritual value should be in every part of each service, sermon, prayers, lessons, music, so that the worshiper shall go away impressed with a single direct phase of truth.

The preacher who would have his sermon gain its full and free effect will give care to the selection of readings and will also prepare to read them effectively from the desk. It is painful to record the fact that more often than not when I have heard ministers read from the Bible in public worship, there has been some slip, some error in emphasis, some hesitation or stumbling, some obscuring of the plain sense, which has given unmistakable evidence that the reader had not carefully read through and thought through and studied through the passage in advance, with a view to making the reading of it take hold of the heart and conscience of the hearer with full power. And sometimes it has been my privilege to hear the Word read so forcibly, so luminously, with such plain intelligence and feeling, that it was like a kindly light shining in the dark. How can we expect people to take seriously our claim that the Bible is the Word of God, and of unique value for the spiritual life, if they find us careless and dull and uninspired in the public presentation of it? I once heard the Scripture read in a Scotch church, by a Scottish minister, in so beautiful, reverent, illuminative a fashion that I should have felt richly fed and served, had there been nothing more to the worship that morning. I once dropped in to hear a famous English preacher, and carried away as the best gain from the service a matchless reading of the Parable of the Prodigal Son. I fear there are few American ministers who make the reading of the Bible stand out as an event in the worship. Every one of us could, and should.

Of course, there are varieties of gifts. Some have voice and manner lacking to others. But any man fit to stand in the pulpit can, if he will, present the Word of God to his people in a way that will be helpful and impressive.

To do this, one must have a good general familiarity with the Biblical material. He must spend time with that version of it from which he reads at the Sunday worship. He must read thoughtfully, and meditate upon it. It will save much time in the end if a minister, at the outset of his ministerial life, will go through a systematic course of Bible study and reading, which will give him for all time a background of knowledge of the varied material therein. This ought

to be given him in the theological school. But if it is
not he should win it for himself early in his ministry. To be able readily, out of such a rich store of
knowledge, to select the passage best suited to a particular occasion or subject will save him very often
either from the necessity of long searching, or from the
tragedy of an inappropriate lesson. Freedom in the
use of the treasures of Biblical truth is a possession
richly worth gaining.

Care in this particular portion of the weekly worship is seen to be of especial importance when one
realizes how little contact with the Bible is the lot of
even the favored youth of the present day. To many
this is the one regular means of coming into touch with
the treasures of God's Word. Is it not richly worth the
expenditure of time and patience necessary to make
this brief reading from the Bible impressive and at-
tractive to all who hear, so that it shall open their
eyes to behold the wondrous things in God's Word?

It is only a sloven who, in his desire to give unity
to the service, will always read the passage in which
his text is found. Often a far stronger impression is
created by the reading of a passage which, from a different angle, and with a different emphasis, unfolds
and enforces the same principle or ideal as that in the
text. The wise minister will have in mind, or on paper,
a list of the best passages, which lend themselves well
to public reading, with which he is so familiar that he
can readily seize on one or another as suitable for a
particular occasion.

One must not easily assume that the unity of the
service should always be secured by ranging all details about the sermon and its theme. There are oc-
currences and movements of common interest, which

may well provide the central idea of the worship. The preacher should be ever on the alert for such indications, and ready to shape his sermon to fit this unifying idea. If, as we believe, God is revealing Himself in the unfolding life of humanity, how better present Him to people than by emphasizing that in which He reveals Himself day by day?

Public prayer presents to the minister its special problem of ordered freedom. It must be neither an "extemporaneous effusion"—to recall the words of the Westminster Directory—nor a cold form prepared in advance. Every man must find his own way. Two of the most inspiring and helpful leaders in public prayer I know have methods diametrically opposed; one writes his prayers with great care; the other has found that writing hampers him, and goes to the worship on Sunday with but a few thoughts in mind about which the prayer forms itself.

But, differ as individual methods may and must, there are certain great and simple facts which all should take into account.

One of them is that we may well develop, in nonliturgical churches, a far larger use than has been customary of prepared prayers. There is a wealth of devotional material from which a minister may cull prayers useful for certain seasons. Most of us have dull Sundays, when we are in no mood to pray. At such times it is a blessed relief to us, and a spiritual gain to the congregation, if we have at hand forms of prayer, of tried worth, personally selected, which we can use simply and devoutly.

One who would pray worthily and helpfully and with true freedom must be at pains to develop a devotional style. There is a language suited to prayer, and one needs to be at home in it. Here again emerges the necessity of knowing the Bible, for there is no other language so fitted for use in prayer as is the language of our English Bible. One should also familiarize himself with the best devotional literature.

We have something to learn from the silent worship of our friends, the Quakers. No one can have participated in the simple worship of a Friends' Meeting and not feel that there is something there which would enrich our worship could we catch it. One of the great preachers of our time, a man of rare gifts in praying, is making increasing use of a method of prayer in which he indicates one by one, in sentences quietly spoken, objects for which all may well pray, and then leaves, after each sentence, a moment of silence, in which all may present before God that special interest. There is much to be commended in this method; it emphasizes with peculiar force the responsibility of each individual worshiper. It might well come more fully into use in our worship. We have much to learn from the Episcopalian on the one hand, from the Quaker on the other, and from all the varieties of religious experience in between.

But this above all is sure, there is no way to power and worth in public prayer that does not demand sincere practice of prayer in private. One must be a man of communion with God in his own life if he is to help others commune with Him. It is one of the mighty advantages of the ministry that the necessity of leading in public worship keeps a man faithful in the practice of his private fellowship with the Spirit of the Eternal and Unseen.

The preacher should put real thought and considerable time into the selection of hymns. Here is an opportunity for an educational work of real value. A modern hymnal is a rich mine of spiritual treasure, both in hymns and in tunes. Many a minister is content with placer mining, leaving the rich veins unworked. It is amazing, if not shameful, the small range which many a minister allows himself and his people among the great hymns. He forms a little circle of favorites, and contentedly moves around within it.

Some pious folk will chafe, of course, whenever a new hymn is introduced. But with reasonable care to mingle unfamiliar numbers with well-known favorites, a minister can go far in the way of introducing his people to the best treasures of Christian song. His ideal should be that set forth by the Master, bringing forth out of his treasury things new and old, even if there are people who insist that always "the old is better." Such use of the hymnal will necessitate on his part a familiarity with the hymnal comparable to that urged in the case of the Bible. One of the first concerns of a minister should be to know thoroughly the hymn-book used in the church he is to serve. Even the busiest minister may well put one or two hours a week into selection of hymns, and study of the hymnal.

It is a serious question, to which every one who believes in the value of public worship, and longs to see it come to its full power over our common social life, should give prolonged and careful attention,—whether we have not come to a time when we need to investigate, with patience and care and open-mindedness, our whole theory and practice of public worship, with a view to changes, perhaps of a very radical sort. There is many a church, in the denominations that call themselves free, Congregational, Presbyterian, Baptist, and the like, that is slavishly bound to inherited ways of worship that are bald and cold and unbeautiful. There is need of open and courageous revisal of our ways and forms, that our worship may be *truly* free—free to range through the rich fields of spiritual experience and its expression by masters of the art of worship. I am not truly *free* in my worship, if I am not free *to use* the treasures of Common Prayer, of art, of music, of symbolism.

One may well be modest and careful about venturing into this new field with confident and detailed suggestions. Many souls must work at the problem, there must be many experiments, some failures, much collaboration, before we shall find the way to a worship at once free and rich. But two specific predictions I am willing to make. One is that we must find ways of producing and maintaining a spiritual atmosphere in our worship; the other is that we must give larger recognition and place to music.

As a whole, our Protestant worship lacks atmosphere. We are afraid of effect, and we are afraid of *silence*. There must always be something *going on*. We forget too easily the voice which says, "Be still, and know that I am God." Our church services suggest too often a program of things to be done, one after the other, with a certain business-like precision. The very manner in which many a minister enters the pulpit discourages rather than enhances the spirit of reverence. The preacher should constantly remind himself that his conduct in the pulpit may be as potent a force in drawing the souls of men toward God or driving them from God as any spoken word. I do not like to speak of the sins of my brethren; but it is a simple and sad fact that seldom have I attended a meeting for public worship at which several ministers were seated together on a platform, that the reverential atmosphere of the service has not been hurt, or ruined, by the lack of reverent attitude, by whispered conversations, inattention, obvious interest in people entering, or passing of notes. Everything that needs to be said or done by way of preparation should be said or done in advance; and from the time those who are to conduct the worship enter the church they should be reverent and silent, as men who know they are in the presence of God.

Every possible precaution should be taken in advance against the intrusion of anything that would mar the atmosphere and spirit of the service. The worship in some churches is conducted in a spirit of cheerful bustle; a hymn is announced as if it had just occurred to the minister that it would be a good thing to sing a hymn at that particular moment, and he had happily hit on just the right hymn to be sung; and he probably announces it by asking the atrocious question, "Shall we sing the 151st hymn?"—a question I never hear without mentally expecting, and almost hoping, to hear some sturdy worshiper shout back, "We shall not!"

Tennyson was right when he said that as knowledge grows to more and more, more of *reverence* should in us dwell. We of the free churches must learn how to make our public worship a source of the spirit of reverence which our American life so sorely needs and lacks. We must have quiet places in our worship, times of silence, an organ interlude after a prayer, brief opportunities for meditation, and over all must brood the spirit of reverential quiet which can be maintained only if the preacher himself leads the people in it, is himself quiet and reverential, conducts every detail of the worship as in the presence of the Most High God.

The second assured fact for the future of worship is that we must give far larger place to music. We must give it more adequate recognition, support, and opportunity.

There are few matters in the realm of church life and practice as to which I am so ready to prophesy confidently as that the future will show a very great increase in the use and value of music in our worship. Music will cease to be a mere ornament, an attraction, a concession to the desire to be entertained, and will become more and more a chosen means of worship which can do for us what no other means can do.

There are clear reasons ~~why~~ music, in itself, and because of its essential nature, is fitted to render a unique religious ministry just now. Music has four qualities, which give it peculiar power in the religious life of the present age, and will make it increasingly useful in the further development of the religious life. It is vital, symbolic, communal, and catholic. And the religious spirit of our time is marked by those very four qualities.

It is characteristic of religion to-day that it is vital. It lays stress on experience. Religion means life, real life; we seek in it a help in living our life now in the flesh. Religion is less and less concerned with the past, as past. It is concerned with present experience of life with God, and with man.

Now music is unique among the arts, almost unique among the common practices of the human spirit, in that it is vital in its very essence. It has not come down to us from the past; it must live and move in our presence. Raphael and Titian left us great works of art, to be set in galleries and museums. We want to see their own work, not any reproductions of it.

But no musical composer ever left a work of art. We do not care to see his original manuscript, except from an instinct of reverent curiosity. Bach and Beethoven have left us not works of art at all, but directions for producing works of art. When we would get the best these masters left us, we do not go to galleries and museums. We go where organs and choruses and soloists and orchestras set these works before us in living, pulsing reality. The musical scores of the great masters are nothing more than their notes, saying: "This is how I made my music. Make it live again."

Where else can one find a more perfect type of religion, as we think of it, and desire it to-day? The Bible is not an art gallery; it is rather a collection of musical scores, directions for living. The supreme concern is that we make the music which the Word of God shows us how to make, that we sing over afresh, with our own voices, the song with which Jesus inspired the world. Religion is vital, as music is vital. It must be set forth in terms and means of present living experience, or it has no more value than have the scores of the great symphonies, set away on a shelf. The whole value of religion is in its vitality, and music is its perfect type.

Music also fits with peculiar power the religion of to-day, because it is essentially symbolic in character. It expresses what lies beyond words.

Unquestionably the religion of to-day craves more and more a medium that goes beyond logic and definition. There is prevalent what Donald Hankey so well called "The religion of the inarticulate." The soul of our time is full of "fancies that break through language and escape." Men feel themselves in the presence of infinite and unfathomable realities, which are dwarfed and cramped in precise creeds and forms of words. Yet some expression must be given or the soul remains unsatisfied.

What can meet this need as can music? The sacrament helps. We should make more use of its values. We should be eager to make room for a greatly enlarged use of symbolism, all through the life of the church. But music has a peculiar if not a unique function in this regard. Who knows what music is? It defies definition or description. Yet nothing more vividly and certainly *is;* and somehow it expresses emotions and soul-experiences which words try in vain to define.

Music also is essentially communal in nature, and therein fits the religion of our day. Christianity is becoming conscious of its social meaning and outworking. A reaction is setting strongly against the overdeveloped individualism of Protestantism. We see that religion is a community matter.

What is there in our life that can so well express this communal instinct as does our singing together or playing together some great product of musical art? It is interesting to pick up one book after another dealing with current social problems, and find that the most common and appropriate illustration of the coöperation needed in a business, a community, or a world, is an orchestra, in which each man plays his own instrument, but all produce harmony. To exalt the music in our churches is to further in' the readiest way the progress of social religion, the sense that no Christian lives to himself, but that each is part of a "beloved community," through which we realize our oneness with God in Christ.

Our religion to-day is catholic in spirit, impatient of disunity. And nothing in our practice of religion so emphasizes this catholicity as does our music. Our creeds divide us; our organizations are fences; even the Sacrament holds us apart, to our shame be it said. But when we sing we are all one. Congregations which would be scandalized were a Catholic priest or a Unitarian minister brought in to lead the worship sing with unalloyed joy Faber's hymn, "There's a Wideness in God's Mercy" or Holmes' splendid "Sun-Day" hymn, "Lord of All Being, Throned Afar." And even more catholic than the hymns is the music to which they are set. Christians in Asia and Africa sing words utterly unintelligible to us. But we catch the tune, and our hearts join with theirs in the emotions awakened and the associations recalled by "Jesus, Lover of My Soul," or "Rock of Ages, Cleft for Me." Music is a universal language, needing no translation, needing only living interpreters to make it live in our presence. How can church unity be better set forward than by giving larger place to music, until the church shall sing its way into its ideal, of "The Holy Catholic Church, the Communion of Saints"?

So music stands out, the best vehicle for religious truth and beauty, especially fitted to the deep and painful needs of an age groping after a God too great to be set in precise words. The most inspired preacher must bow his head in the presence of music, as the English poet did, recognizing that

Here is the finger of God, a touch of the will that can,
Existent behind all laws, that made them, and lo! they are;
And I know not if, save in this, such gift be allowed to man,

That out of three sounds he frame, not a fourth sound, but
  a star.
Consider it well, each tone of our scale in itself is naught;
It is everywhere in the world, loud, soft, and all is said.
Give it to me to use, I mix it with two in my thought;
And, there! Ye have seen and heard. Consider, and bow
  the head.

It has seemed right to give larger space to the discussion of the value and place of music than to that of
any other element in worship, not only because of the
peculiarly powerful appeal which music makes to-day
to the soul of man; but also because it is an element in
our worship that has never received adequate recognition and attention. We preachers have tended to look
at it rather as a pleasing adjunct to worship, an appeal
to the lower nature, or even as a necessary evil, than
as one of the noblest and most effective means of developing in the soul of man, and expressing for that
soul, the instinct of worship. We have suffered severely from the Protestant propensity to deify talk.
It may chasten the spirit of the preacher, and help him
to a better mind, to realize that such glimpses as the
Bible affords into the glory of the life to come show
us never a sermon, but many a song; a city of God
without a temple, but never without music. The true
city of God is like that magic city of Arthur of which
Tennyson tells us that it was "Built to music, therefore never built at all, and therefore built forever."
No one is making, or beginning to make, full use of
his ministry, who is not doing his utmost to give music
the largest possible place in the life and worship of
the church. Few ministers and churches begin to take
music seriously as an agent of religion. One of the
most neglected opportunities in this country is to be

found in the many church organs silent save for a few minutes each week, and indifferently handled then. Music should be ranked with preaching and teaching, as one of the three indispensable elements of the worship and life of a church.

In a certain church in a great city there is held every noon a simple service of worship. From thirty to a hundred and fifty people attend. But once a week that noon hour is wholly given to music; and then the church is crowded to its utmost capacity, and often hundreds are turned away. No one who watches that throng can possibly think that the difference is due entirely, or even very largely, to the fact that the people enjoy entertainment more than they delight in the worship of God. The explanation is rather that they find in music an expression of their desire for fellowship with God, a voicing of their ideals and aspirations, an instrument of worship, more appealing, more helpful, than they find in words of prayer and exhortation. Sidney Lanier, who knew better than most the meaning both of music and of religion, gave a definition as true as it is beautiful, when he said, "Music is love in search of a word." Is not that descriptive of the religion of many a soul to-day? It is "Love in search of a word." Is it strange if music appeals to us as no other voice or form can do?

> For love well knows he never may express
> In words a tithe of all his tenderness;
> But music is a house not made with hands,
> Built by love's Father, where a little space
> The soul may dwell; a royal palace fit
> To meet the majesty of its demands;
> The place where man's two lives unite; the place
> To hold communion with the infinite.

One concrete inference from a realization of the value of music in religion is that we should give to the leader of the music in a church far greater recognition as a religious leader than has ever been given. The director of music should be set apart by some simple service of recognition comparable with the ordination of a minister. He should be looked upon as an associate in religious leadership. We should no more think of setting over the music of a church a man lacking in religious faith and experience, however great an artist, than we would think of putting into the pulpit a man lacking in religious experience and faith, however brilliant an orator. The first requirement for the director of music in a church should be that he be a man of God.

Between him and the minister should be maintained the most cordial, intimate, and continuous coöperation. If the minister is by temperament unmusical, let him trust implicitly in the guidance of the director, imparting to him constantly his own earnest religious spirit, ever counting him an indispensable associate. If the minister is blessed with a musical nature, there are rich possibilities of combined ministry, which will make his preaching immensely more effective. His best sermons will be given wings by the fitting music that surrounds them; and many a sermon will spring out of the music itself.

So here, as everywhere, the preacher finds the best and truest freedom by gladly inserting his free spirit within this network of necessity, this elaborate combination of Scripture-reading, and prayer, and song, and anthem and organ-playing, which seems to demand of him so much time and care that he longs to give to the preparation and delivery of his message.

The more he seeks to fit his sermon into the worship, the more he gives time and sympathy and enlarged place to the symbolical elements of the worship, and the musical expression of devotion, the more will he find his way as a preacher into the truer, higher liberty wherein the whole truth and beauty of God is set free in the soul and society of man.

CHAPTER IV

THE CHURCHMAN

EVERY man of the right sort who enters the ministry longs to spend himself altogether on high levels of thinking and action, free from all the clinging garments of tradition, and all the rigid ways of institutionalism. More young men than we imagine wish they might preach in the fields as Jesus did, or in the streets and by the way as St. Francis did, free from responsibility to any organization. The desire to escape from the institutional and to live wholly in the vital and spiritual is doubtless more widely and deeply felt to-day than for decades or centuries past.

But, wish this as he may, the minister finds it a dream hard to realize. It fades in the cold light of facts. If he is to fill a preacher's place in the church, there is a local congregation, with its ways and thoughts and traditions, into which he must fit. Moreover, there is a denominational connection to be seriously held, and maintained, by the congregation and the minister. Whether we like it or not, the fact is that Christianity is institutionally organized; and that means that, for the vast mass of preachers,— with exceptions so few that they may be disregarded, —one must adapt himself and his ideals to the thoughts and habits, the intellectual and practical requirements, of a local congregation, and of a particular denomination with which it is connected.

True of the homeland, this is at least equally true of Christian service abroad. Mission work is institutionally organized. And one must demonstrate his general loyalty to the points of view and ways of working which characterize the particular denomination under the patronage of which he is to do his work. There is a growing tendency to standardization and unity, yet along with it goes a startling reaction to denominational loyalty. It may be long before the various parts of the Christian Church will abandon their particular demands for conformity on the part of those who would enter their service, at home or abroad.

Here then is a mass of creeds, forms, customs, traditions, into which a preacher comes. How shall he maintain his freedom in the midst of it all? Nay, rather, how shall he find it possible to insert his freedom within this necessity, and turn it to his profit?

The cases are very few where one may well venture to take his lonely way, unconnected with any institutional form of Christianity, quite irresponsible. Livingstone was right in severing connection with mission boards; but Livingstone was a man in a million, with a clear call to a definite work which, plainly, could be better done in absolute freedom. And Livingstone, be it well remembered, did not break with the institution until he had served under it for long years, and saw a clear path to greater usefulness through severing the relationship.

On the whole it may be said that the men who hold aloof from denominational and institutional connection lose power thereby enormously. Usually they cripple their usefulness. I know a young man of the finest type, financially independent, devoted in soul to the missionary ideal, so set on keeping free from the trammels of denominational control that he will not serve under any Board of Missions. The net result of that attitude,—admirable in its motive as it is,—has been to keep him irresolute and idle for several years. He is still undecided how and where to go ahead, while comrades of his, duller in mind, less ardent in spirit, far more poorly endowed internally and externally, have found their way into satisfying usefulness and worthy results.

For that sort of freedom one can easily pay too high a price. It might be a truer way of putting it to say that such a man is in reality less free than he would be through reasoned and cordial conformity to some organized branch of the Christian church. He would be submitting to limitations on his liberty, he says, by such a course. Is not his freedom limited by the lack of opportunity to which he condemns himself by his isolation,—limited too in the most serious way, for he is less free to do good honest work for the Kingdom of God?

Unless a man has a direct and unmistakable call of God to a task which can unquestionably be better done independently of all institutions, he will be more free, more honest, more successful, more useful, for cordial and loyal affiliation with some organized church body. He will have regrets, of course; he must make delicate adjustments between his individuality and the traditions and beliefs of his institution; his honesty will be more open to question, more difficult to maintain; but all that is a part of life. Life gets forward when freedom is willing to insert itself within necessity, when free spirits stay with the established order of things and carry it all on to better thoughts, truer convictions, wider views, and sounder ways.

It is especially hard in our day for the preacher to conform, because of the revolution that has taken place in the forms of our religious thought. True though it be that "every age is an age of transition," there do come certain times when the distance between vanguard and rear is greatly extended, when it is peculiarly hard for those who have caught the new view and those content with the old, to get on well together. We may venture to hope with some confidence that we are getting out of the fierce fight between old and new theology, that a reasonable modernism has won its right to real respect in the church; that the present upflaring of theological reaction is only the last effort of a dying cause; yet we are in the penumbra of the struggle; and it is still hard for one trained to look at life from the modern viewpoint to live comfortably with those who cling to older thoughts and ways. It is one of the most perplexing and vexing questions, what are the rightful limits of personal independence of thought on the one hand, and accommodation to the thoughts and ways of a congregation or a denomination on the other?

It is not, as it is so often represented as being, a simple question of honesty. That would be an easy matter. It is the far more difficult and delicate question, how far one should give weight to his individual judgments and opinions, how far fit into the general thought and feeling of certain groups with which he must work. One should never say that he believes what he does not believe; one must be honest and sincere, at whatever cost. Of course; that is the abc of action. But one is not a preacher simply in order to

make clear to the world exactly what he individually
believes and thinks. What does the world care for his
individual opinion? Society gets forward not because
some men get outside and shout their individual convictions, but, far more, because a great many men stay
inside and keep their convictions quietly and forcibly
and progressively at work among relationships held
unbroken. "Like a mighty army moves the church of
God"; the analogy is far from perfect, but there is
truth in it. And it is not a mighty army, but a mighty
poor army, in which every man acts with absolute independence, and refuses to submit his freedom to the
yoke of discipline.

This is one of the hardest and most important problems for every preacher, to work out the rightful
limits of freedom and conformity, so that he will be
neither a slave to his congregation or his denomination, nor a free lance tilting at it. If there is one fact
clear to-day it is that success demands the maximum
development of team work. Other things being any-
where near equal, the man who can manage to work
with reasonable freedom within the institution of the
church will accomplish ten times as much as the man
who can keep free only by remaining unrelated.

How shall one solve this problem? Each must solve
it for himself. Yet there are certain common features
of the problem which may helpfully be discussed in a
general way.

This problem of freedom and conformity naturally
falls into a twofold division. It presses upon the
preacher in the two fields of *thought* and *act*. We
limit our attention to the former, reserving the matter
of freedom of action in ecclesiastical affairs to the next
chapter.

The question we are discussing relates to one's thoughts, his beliefs, his intellectual approach to Christianity. How can one, while preserving his honesty and candor unstained, and his liberty of thought unviolated, yet maintain working relations with those who differ with him, and loyalty to his denomination?

Let us make the approach to it very concrete. Here is a young man, trained in a good theological school. That means that he has caught and cordially adopted something at least of the modern point of view in theology, Biblical criticism, psychology, religious education, and the rest. He is called to minister to a congregation of the average sort. There are good people there, an overwhelming majority of them, whose hearts are right, whose motives are good, whose piety is real. There are, perhaps, a few trouble-makers, people who watch for causes of offense. There are many untrained minds so far as theology is concerned, who hold simply and without much question a faith given to them in earlier days. There are men who, because they have been successful in business, think they have a right to pronounce positively on questions of theology. There are some also whose religion is like that of Dr. Kennicott in "Main Street," of whom the author says, "He believed in the church, but seldom attended its services. He believed in Christianity, but never thought about it. He was worried over Carol's lack of faith, but was not sure just what it was she lacked." Be sure there are also in the congregation young people, and some older ones, who have found the old forms of belief increasingly unsatisfying, and are longing for light on the way to beliefs which they can honestly hold and on which their soul's life can depend. There are also children to be so influenced that they shall grow normally into forms and ways of thought and belief that shall be natural and satisfying for the day in which they must live their lives. There are students, away at college, needing to be held in strong relationship to the institutional church.

— Into this congregation comes as preacher a man who has been trained in the latest and best view of Christian truth, to whom now is given the wonderful opportunity of helping all these people to think and to believe, of leading them into thoughts of God and of life ever better and truer, of developing the congregation into a power house of Christian thought and feeling. What shall he do? If he is insincere, he will lose them all. But, on the other hand, if he has that overtrained sincerity which is at heart self-assertion, and obstinate independence, he will hold and lead but a small group, and those the ones who need it least.

What should he do?

First of all, he must cheerfully and courageously defend his right and duty to state the Gospel in terms adapted to the modern mind. His motive in so doing need not be, and should not be, the defense of his personal right to liberty of thought. He should assume that, not claim it. His motive should be a missionary motive, an eager desire to present Christian truth in terms that shall give it power over those who need it most. Whenever there comes a choice between the comfort of the contented and the winning of the troubled, the true preacher will not hesitate. Better a thousand times to disturb the placidity of old and settled believers than to fail to minister to young and questioning souls. Any good shepherd will neglect the ninety and nine who are safe-folded, and go after that which is lost. And the youth of our time are lost, not as the prodigal was, but as the sheep was, bewildered, caught between the demands of a rigid orthodoxy in the church and a no less rigid agnostic philosophy in the college and university. It is one of the supreme functions and privileges of the preacher of to-day to put the Gospel in terms intelligible to the modern student.

In the Bible itself is a magnificent illustration of the power of such reinterpretation of essential religion in terms to meet a new and urgent need. We never should have had the Fourth Gospel had not its author dared to restate the life of Christ in terms fitted to meet the new and prevalent philosophy of his time. It was an appeal to what was then modern thought. Here was a world thinking in terms of the "Logos," while Christianity up to that time had been cast in terms of the "Messiah." What should be done? Cling to the Messianic terminology as divinely ordained and unchangeable, let what might happen to the world at large? Doubtless there were good souls of orthodox Jewish antecedents who insisted on the duty of talking the more in terms of Messianism the less intelligible and real those terms became. They called it loyalty to the faith once delivered to the saints. But this great soul spoke out in terms of the thinking of his time, interpreting Jesus as the Eternal Word, the light of life, rather than as the fulfillment of racial dreams; changing the scene of His promised coming from the clouds of heaven to the spiritual life of the race. By bravely and brilliantly rethinking and restating the meaning of Christ and His Gospel in terms of current philosophy, he gave a new impetus to Christianity which it feels to-day and will feel forever. Let the thinker and the preacher of to-day be as eager and as forceful in restating the essentials of Christianity in terms that shall appeal to minds swayed by the conceptions of modern science and the philosophy of evolution as John was in appealing to minds swayed by Alexandrian philosophy and Oriental mysticism.

Let the preacher take for granted the right and duty of appealing to the modern mind in the name of Christ. Let him clearly show his congregation that it is vastly more important to "hold knowledge and religion together," for the young than to leave the old undisturbed in their traditional inheritance. Let him say with Paul, when in similar circumstances, "From henceforth let no man trouble me."

But let him be sure he can finish the sentence, "For I bear in my body the marks of the Lord Jesus." Let it be clear beyond the shade of a possible doubt that he is ever acting and speaking in the spirit of Christ, and for the sake of the spirits of men.

The preacher must realize,—most of all if he be of the modern and liberal sort, that he is a missionary to souls, not a propagandist for ideas. Let him remind himself of it over and over, let him keep it before himself every moment of his ministry—that the main element in true religious experience is not the intellectual construction of religion, but the practice of it.

That will not mean that he will despise or neglect the intellectual construction. Every true preacher will be constantly training his congregation in theology; his ministry will be seriously defective otherwise. But it will, and it does, mean that he will always hold intellectual development, and theological correctness, clearly subordinate to the development of spiritual experience. He will give expression to his own theological convictions only as such expression will help forward the spiritual aim and object he has in view in the sermon.

He will quickly give, and steadily maintain, in his preaching, the impression of one who cares first of all for the spiritual development and upbuilding of the people set in his care. He will want most of all, and through all, to build them up in Christ Jesus, to help them forward, and to go forward with them, into an ever-ripening, ever-enlarging, never-ending appropriation of what God has for His Children in the Gospel, and in the life of which the Gospel is the supreme interpretation,—the life of the Spirit.

One who stands in the pulpit every Sunday in that attitude, so that no one can mistake his primary spiritual aim, can always voice his convictions freely and fearlessly. It may be laid down as an absolute law, that, given clear confidence on the part of the hearers that the speaker seeks first their spiritual upbuilding, that his main concern is with the spiritual life and not with the propagation of certain views, and he can say anything he honestly believes, and carry the wholesome respect and attention of practically all in the congregation. With this primary and steadfast regard for spiritual experience and growth must go,—indeed it is a vital part of it,—tender and thoughtful consideration for every person in the congregation, in the form in which the truth is presented. Here is the place where many fail. They confuse loyalty to their convictions with rigidity of language.

I know certain apostles of modern faith who boast that they have discarded the familiar terminology of the church. They will not use the words "atonement," "salvation," and the like. They call their attitude honesty. It is not. It is the foolish, unnecessary, and unjustifiable casting away of a great asset. The right spirit is that of Jesus, who came "not to destroy, but to fulfil"; it is right in line with His mission to take these old words, and fulfil them, fill them full of timely meanings, raise them from the dead and set them to living and working again.

Just as the greatest poet is not the one who scorns common terminology and goes afar in search after new words and conceits of literary form; but rather the one who can express the profoundest realities in the simplest of common words; so the truest preacher is not he who will smite his people in the face with new expressions and phrases, but rather he who will make time-honored and precious and simple words and phrases glow with life, and serve as the vehicles of the ever-growing teaching of the Spirit, Who guides us into all the truth.

A minister of my acquaintance had lately come to a certain congregation. The church was a conservative one; the man was of the progressive, or modern type. Shortly after his coming, he became aware that many of the younger people were having serious trouble over the Bible. They could not take it any longer in the old literal fashion; they knew no other definite way in which to take it. They were disturbed and over-awed by the dominance of the conservative view.

To meet this need, he preached one Sunday on the modern view of the Bible. He began by saying that he supposed most of the members of the congregation were quite satisfied with their inherited view of the Bible. But he had found a considerable number who had felt constrained, under the force of their necessary thinking in other lines, to abandon, or change radically, their old view of the Bible as inerrant. He asked permission to address this special group, to show them what was left to them, what the authority and value of the Bible might still be to them, even if they took an extreme modern view of it. He then frankly discussed the matter, outlining the essentials of the modern view of the Bible, pointing out how little one loses in giving up the idea of a magically inerrant book; how actually there may be positive gains in a more human and natural view of the Hebrew Scriptures; and ended by emphasizing the abiding values of the Bible, which hold through all shiftings of formal theory about its inspiration.

When the service was over, one of his hearers, himself a minister of modern mind, said to him, "I was thinking how so-and-so (naming a brilliant man of very radical attitude) would have preached that sermon. He would have meant just what you meant. But he would have begun by declaring, 'It is now generally admitted that the Bible is not the Word of God,' and would have had his congregation by the ears at once."

In this case, the preacher gained the sympathy of all at the outset, by clearly affirming a spiritual aim, a missionary motive, for the discussion. He carried through the whole sermon a constructive attitude and a reverent temper. He spoke of old forms of faith with respect, not with contempt or ridicule. The result was that, without a shadow of insincerity, without any covering over of his convictions, he won and kept the sympathetic interest of all, and left the most reactionary of his hearers more generously inclined toward modern views of the Bible. A congregation faced in that spirit will insensibly grow into a larger faith.

"Speaking the truth in Love,"—that is a simple phrase, but a wonderfully good motto. The preacher who speaks every Sunday, unmistakably, from a great desire to serve the souls of the people, and with living consideration for their point of view, will seldom if ever have cause to complain that he is not free to tell the truth about God and life and theology as he sees these great realities. He may not be free to speak out all that he privately thinks. Why should he? To take the pulpit as a soap-box, whence one may cry his own individual opinions, is insufferable egotism. The true preacher will not want to use his pulpit for expressing any of his views save those which will make a vital difference in the spiritual experience of his congregation. He will have enough to occupy him if he keeps within those limits. It is foolish to stray outside them, seeking a freedom which is in truth a restriction.

Ministers of modern mind are sometimes greatly exercised over the repeating of the Apostles' Creed, as part of the worship in their congregations. The case we have in mind and need to discuss is not that in which a congregation is facing the question whether to adopt the practice of reciting the creed each Sunday, or at special services. Nor are we dealing with the question whether it is well to repeat any creed as a part of worship, or whether some simpler or more satisfying creed cannot be found.

We are dealing with a fact; that fact is that there are still many churches in which the repetition of the Apostles' Creed is a part of the regular order of worship; and many persons value it highly as an expression of the community of faith in the church, and as a solemn act in which all can readily take part.

What should be the attitude of the minister of modern mind toward this part of the worship? It is perfectly plain, of course, that the man who positively disbelieves the major affirmations of that Creed ought not to join in repeating it. But any man who does not believe really and heartily in God the Father, in Jesus Christ, in the Holy Spirit, in the church, in forgiveness of sins, and in eternal life, ought not to be in the pulpit of any Christian church.

But what of the man who, believing these great affirmations, is in doubt about certain minor words and phrases; uncertain about the literal truth of alleged facts, in the past; indifferent as to whether Christ was or was not born of a virgin; repelled by the materialistic import of such a phrase as "the resurrection of the body"; or impressed with the inadequacy of a creed which omits the Kingdom of God, and certain other important truths? What shall he do?

I have known preachers, under such conditions, who insisted that the creed be eliminated from the worship when they were to lead it; or who left the leading in it to some other, and stood silent during the act. I cannot see how they can, in the name of liberty and honesty, so grossly intrude their personal likes and idiosyncrasies upon an ordered worship. If the pastor of a church honestly believes that the recitation of the creed is harmful rather than helpful to the spiritual life of the people, let him take up the matter with the officers and people to get it elided from the service quietly in good time and in good temper. But, so long as it forms part of the accepted order of the worship, and he is in hearty accord with its major affirmations, let him devoutly take his part in the recitation of it.

Is the personal preference, or point of view, of one man, and that on minor points, to decide what form the combined expression of congregational worship shall take? The recitation of the creed, at a church service, is not an expression of individual belief; it is an act of worship. If it were what some seem to think it, a theological test thrust into the midst of the worship, it would be insufferable. But it is clearly intended as an act of worship, exactly as are the hymns, the reading of the Scriptures, and the other acts. The recitation of the creed is an acknowledgment that Christians share in a great common faith, which has been given a great common and simple form. We rise and recite this faith of the church, as an imperfect statement, not adequately setting forth the views of any individual Christian; but the best we can find in which all may take part. To refuse to repeat it because one does not accept every article of it as part of his private and personal belief, is a hysterical individualism, quite one with the practice in which some oversensitive worshipers indulge,—of searching each hymn to make sure that it represents exactly what they believe, else they will not join in the singing of it. This is Protestantism become a disease, an exaggeration of one's little personal experience into a wall to shut one's self from all large and generous coöperation in common experience. The proper totem for all that tribe is Kipling's "Cat that Walks by Himself," and it is the symbol of a passing phase of Protestantism.

In addition to the adjustment of the preacher to his local congregation, its beliefs and customs, there is necessary also some adaptation of the minister to that particular branch of the church with which he is immediately connected. Most of our Protestant denominations demand that candidates submit to certain theological tests, or require subscription to particular creeds.

With the rapid advance of theological knowledge, and the growth of independent thinking, it is becoming increasingly hard for ministers heartily to subscribe to any ancient form of words as the confession of their personal faith. Many have come to see that creed subscription is an anomaly, and to question if it be not a huge mistake to base church fellowship and organization, and to determine good standing in the ministry, on intellectual conformity. There are many of us who are sure that the church would be immensely stronger and sounder if the basis of fellowship and good standing were made a matter of real faith, of purpose and spirit, and if the intellectual form of one's belief were left and encouraged to be free. In short the church should have a spiritual rather than a creedal basis.

But the great body of the Christian church is at present on a basis of creed subscription. What shall the minister of the modern type in thought and attitude do in such a situation? It is the same problem which he confronts everywhere. It is easy for the uncompromising radical, who frankly casts away the evangelical faith. Let him be non-conformist, and glory in it. It is easy also for the man at the other extreme, whose faith naturally takes on forms like those the fathers used to make. But these extremists are few in number. What of the large body of men who, warmly evangelical in spirit and sympathy, find that seventeenth century language does not well voice their real convictions?

They will be wisest and freest if they make the best of a situation far from ideal, by taking the steps necessary for connection with that denomination of the Christian Church with which they are most heartily in accord, in its spirit, traditions, and ways of working. It is well understood that the terms of subscription in all our denominations are far from being ironclad. They imply a general attitude rather than a particular endorsement. Moreover, the outstanding creeds to which subscription is asked are themselves characterized by a certain largeness and generosity of spirit, or even hold within themselves variations of wide range. Take what may justly be called the most outstanding of Protestant creeds, the Westminster Confession of Faith. It is clear to any student of it that that document contains two clearly differentiated strands of thought,—the legal and the vital, the formal and the spiritual. One could go through it, tracing the two tendencies, and emerge with two documents, as decisively marked as of different spiritual origin as are the Priestly and the Deuteronomic elements in the Hexateuch. If the conservative forces insist that subscription to such a creed involves full acceptance of its formal and literal views, the liberal forces can with equal right insist that subscription involves frank and full acceptance of its spiritual and vital principles, which play havoc with literalism.

Under such conditions, a man of real evangelical spirit, whose beliefs take on modern forms, may well with great cheerfulness, and with unclouded soul, subscribe to such an ancient document as a means to fellowship and service in that body of the church with which he is most naturally in sympathy. To insist on remaining free by refusing to subscribe is to retain the form of freedom while losing its real meaning and value.

The church is, first of all, and beyond all, a working fellowship, a missionary body. One who has true Christian faith and zeal in his soul wants to work with that body. He may well, to that end, agree to limit somewhat his absolute liberty of theological statement, and to adhere to ancient forms of words not wholly suited to his thoughts; meanwhile working steadily, as in all loyalty he may and should, towards a better and simpler form of creed or of creed subscription, or toward the laying aside of formal creeds as a basis of church fellowship, and the substitution of a statement of loyalty to Christ and to the ideals of the Gospel.

An incident from the ecclesiastical history of a generation ago may have value. During the conduct of a noted heresy trial in the Presbyterian church, a resolution was introduced in the General Assembly of that denomination, declaring that the Bible is free from error. An amendment was offered, declaring that the doctrine of Holy Scripture as contained in the Westminster Confession, is satisfactory and adequate. The amendment was defeated, clearly proving that the reactionary party then in power in that church was in reality trying, not to enforce the accepted standards, but to impose a view not found in the standards. This is but one decisive bit of evidence of the large liberty to be found in ancient creeds, the freedom that exists within the elements of subscription to a varied confession of belief.

No one with any regard for progress, or with anything of the Christian spirit and outlook, would urge that any one should stifle or cramp honest convictions, or profess a faith he does not share, or purchase fellowship and recognition by intellectual or practical dis-

honesty. But any one capable of large and true views
will see that creed subscription is, by nature and of
necessity, a compromise, in which men and groups
of differing views unite on a common statement which
on the whole serves to set forth the great principles on
which they agree to work; that every form of words is
susceptible of different interpretations, and that sub-
scribers reserve personal liberty of choice among the
varieties of interpretation, and, above all, that the right
to work with other Christians in a great, strong, organized fellowship of service may be worth more than
the right to untrammelled liberty in constructing and
stating one's intellectual beliefs. It is a question
whether the soldier, definitely enlisted in the fight for
a noble cause, and thereby brought under definite restrictions of speech and action, is not really a freer
man than the bushwhacker, who

> Won't obey no orders,
> Without they are his own.

There may be a flavor of the sacramental about the
taking of orders. Robertson, Maurice, Kingsley, Bushnell, Beecher, Brooks, these were not only freer than
the small and timid reactionary churchmen who
snapped at their heels, or barked "heretic,"—they were
in fact freer than those who, in the name of freedom,
broke with the church, left its fellowship, started private and independent movements, and lost the inspiration and strength of unity with the great common
organized ongoing of the Christian Church.

It is not easy to be a free man in soul and intellect
and speech and act, and at the same time to be a true
and loyal minister in some branch of the church. One
will be sure to meet suspicion and distrust from both

extremes, and to meet much impugning of motive and of honor. But like all hard courses, most of all those hard courses which hold close to the common heart and the common ways of humanity, and keep vigorous some larger unity, it is a glorious course, very close to that freedom of spirit which was in Christ and is in the true Christian.

CHAPTER V

ONE of the hardest problems the average minister faces is how to be at once a preacher, a pastor and a man of affairs. How can he keep his pulpit work fresh, vigorous, worth while, and at the same time meet the incessant and increasing demands of his parish, his community, his denomination and all the other interests which call upon his time and strength and thought?

What are the proper limits of the freedom of the preacher from pastoral work and administrative detail? How far may he hope to be able to insert his free spirit within these necessities, and actually turn them to its profit?

Here, as elsewhere, the exceptional preacher may be justified in declaring his full independence, and declining to undertake pastoral and administrative work. He may give his church officers, as Dr. Watkinson is said to have done, a choice between his head and his feet, declaring it impossible that they shall have both. The man in the exceptional field may also find a way out, through division of function among a large staff. But such instances do nothing for the average preacher except to arouse feelings of hopeless envy. Such a solution of the problem is like a solution of the problem of domestic service announced by a wealthy woman in Chicago. It consisted in having relays of servants, so maintaining an eight-hour day. She innocently forgot that most homes count themselves fortunate if they can get and keep one or two helpers for the general work of the household.

So the minister in the exceptional field, where resources are abundant, and a large staff is possible, may serenely announce that the problem confronting us can be solved by the application of the principle of division of labor, by which the preacher turns over to others the burden and responsibility for parish and community work. Undoubtedly something may be done through that means. We must come to fewer and larger churches, with a highly differentiated staff, if the church is to play its rightful part. This necessitates, in smaller centers, some outworking of the very interesting and perplexing problem of the "community church." In some way it must be discovered how denominational churches may combine into a real community church, drawing denominational lines into one strong cord, without thereby losing practical and living contact with the great national and international movements of the church. The man who can solve that problem will be one of the great benefactors of the church.

I think we have come, or are coming, to a time which will demand very courageous and decisive action in the way of combinations of churches which shall greatly reduce their number and as greatly increase the power of the units so produced. We have been working at church unity from the top, trying to bring about coalescence of denominations. It may come more surely, and even more swiftly, from the bottom, through the union of churches of various denominations in a town or neighborhood, to produce one strong and adequate church. There are dangers along that way. Much of our present ecclesiastical machinery will be wrecked if the church as a whole takes that path to a solution of the problem of its divisions. But if ever the churches begin to go down that line (and there are signs that they may be drawing near to such a decision) it will be the part of wisdom for denominational Boards and other agencies to adjust their work to the new conditions as rapidly as possible, even at considerable sacrifice. It may be the divine way of removing church unity from the realm of amiable talk into that of actual accomplishment.

But until such a solution comes,—and it is scarcely visible on the horizon as yet,—and to a large extent after it comes,—the bulk of churches must be ministered to very largely each by one man, who must be, to an extent and in ways which might have paralyzed the great apostle himself, "all things to all men."

One who has a real gift for preaching often finds himself longing ineffectively that he might be a preacher and nothing else. But here is his parish; and here come counsels from church officers, and editorials and articles in a ceaseless stream, calling for more pastoral care on the part of the minister, and for a revival of parish visiting; solemnly assuring him that no excellence in the pulpit can make up for neglect of personal contacts with his people. Here is some Forward Movement in his denomination bombarding him each week with demands for a new organization of the men, or women, or children, or young people, or infants, of his congregation. Here are worthy movements and organizations calling for the appointment of a committee on every possible subject; designating the use of one Sunday after another for special purposes, until he finds it hard to make room for any real preaching. Here is his community, with its schools, its charities, its common social enterprises, asking, as it has the right to ask, his practical, sympathetic and considerable service on boards and committees and special undertakings. The benevolent and missionary agencies of his denomination reproach him if he is not continually in a state of full information about all of them, so that he can adequately present them to the congregation, or to individuals, at any time. Here is the fringe about his parish, the people who hang to its edges, the unchurched of the community. Might he not reach them if he gave more time to them? But they demand so much time, the demand of a family for interest and attention varying inversely as the square of the distance between the family and the church life and work.

So this man who would be a preacher finds himself pulled in many ways, all leading out from his study, all taking him away from that quiet of soul, that intensity of thought, that leisure for reading and meditation, which is so vital to worthy work in the pulpit.

The wise preacher will eagerly welcome the largest available measure of volunteer assistance, on the part of the men and women of his congregation. He will do more than welcome; he will foster it, and seek to call it out. No minister is adequately discharging his responsibility for that group of people over whom the Lord has made him overseer who is not doing his utmost to see that they know the joy and worth of rendering real service.

The interest awakened in recent years in the possibilities of laymen's work is of great value to the minister who wants the largest possible measure of relief from the burden of administrative detail. Too often

the preacher fails to trust the laymen of his church
with real responsibility; he will not exert himself to
make the necessary division and differentiation of
tasks and functions; he will not spend himself to inspire them with the desire for real service. It takes
time and grace to make real workmen for God, to
overcome the ready pleas of incapacity, and of lack
of time. It often seems easier for the minister to
shoulder the load than to apportion it among his laymen. But the minister who consistently aims to put
the largest possible amount of responsibility on the
shoulders of the men and women of the congregation
is not only helping them very greatly; he is preparing
the way for his own greater freedom for his own definite work; and he is cultivating among the people of his
parish the needed sense that the minister should be
kept free from matters of business and administration,
to put undivided strength into his spiritual work and
service. The lesson of the sixth chapter of the Acts of
the Apostles might well be taken to heart in many a
church, where the ministers are neglecting the Word of
God and prayer in order to serve tables. The preacher
should definitely expect real service and leadership on
the part of the people, should trust them to furnish it,
and should not too carefully oversee or direct them in
the way they do it. Strong men and women will respond, if called to give real service, and given real and
full authority in the rendering of it.

The problem is not really and wholly solved even
where a minister is fortunate enough to have connected with his church a staff of workers. That may
ease the situation greatly, especially if he be wise
enough to trust his subordinates largely, and to exercise only a general supervision. Otherwise, if he is one

of those men who must oversee every part of the work, he is only the more a slave of administrative detail for every assistant added to his church staff.

But, as we have said, even in the most favored cases, where there is a well-organized staff, with clearly delimited functions, the problem is not solved. For it is the man who speaks from the pulpit who is wanted in other places. It is he whom the community wants, he whom the parishioners wish to see in their homes. And in his heart he knows that they are right; that the preacher must also be the private friend and the public servant.

So emerges a difficult problem, which drives many a man to despair, which makes the ministry a hard calling, even at the best. How can one be a preacher, and yet meet faithfully and capably the demands made upon the minister of a parish?

First of all, he must cultivate, among the people of his parish and his community, a sense of the central importance and dignity of the preaching function. Somehow he must get them to be at one with him in estimating the message from the pulpit as one of the greatest and most vital factors in the life of the church and of the town. He cannot do this unless his pulpit work is of the highest possible order. The man who allows his preparation for preaching to slacken and degenerate through absorption in other work, however good and worthy, is killing his own usefulness. The man who makes his sermons indispensable will speedily have many joining to protect him in that freedom from detailed business which is essential to the best preaching.

Is it not time we were setting ourselves resolutely against the tide of opinion and talk which is running with accelerating pace against the preacher and his business? Men are writing and talking of the passing of the pulpit, of the decadence of preaching. They are telling us that the coming of the journal and the magazine and the book has largely, if not wholly, done away with the necessity and the usefulness of preaching. There is also plainly discernible a rising tide of interest in worship, a sacramentarian tendency, which threatens to submerge the pulpit.

Those of us who believe, what there is every reason for believing, that preaching is one of the permanent factors in religion, and that religion is the greatest factor in individual and social life, should take pains to assert and reassert the dignity and importance of the pulpit. We may and should make way for a great development of the symbolic, for a far larger recognition of the emotions in our public worship, for more music, greater use of the sacrament of the Lord's Supper, and a richer liturgy. But woe to the church if this shall mean a weakening of the pulpit, or acquiescence in a general disparagement of it. When one contemplates on the one hand the bare and chilly devotional atmosphere of our non-liturgical churches, and on the other the thin and careless pulpit work which so often characterizes the liturgical churches, he begins to dream of what the power of the church might be, if once there should arise a church characterized by a union of the two elements, vigorous, thoughtful, passionate preaching set in colorful, heart-moving worship.

Here, as elsewhere, the preacher must maintain himself at the highest level, whatever he may do on other lines also. We must emphasize the importance of the preaching function. The more it is depreciated, the more must we give our souls to it, to make it indispensable and glorious in the sight of men, and to commend it as not wholly unworthy in the sight of God.

Yet, so curiously tangled is the web of life, that in actual practice the minister cannot preach in a way to make people think his sermons indispensable unless he is in thorough and quick contact with the life of the community, and in relations of utmost friendliness with the individuals and homes in his parish. He could hardly make a greater mistake than to try to build up a sense that his sermons are worth while by holding himself aloof from the main currents of the general life. Men and women want to hear a man of their own, who knows their affairs, and is alive to their interests.

But he can so live with them, and work with them, and enter their friendships and their homes, that always they shall think of him as the man with a message, and shall want most of all to save his strength for the pulpit. If he himself has such a conception of the central importance of preaching, and unflinchingly acts on it, others will also come to feel in that way about him and his work.

Help will also come from a constant recognition on his part that his preaching needs the stimulus of personal contact with the people to whom he speaks from the pulpit. Let him say frequently to himself that, were a man free from personal relationships from Sunday to Sunday, coming to the pulpit out of a week of undistracted study, meditation, and writing; he might produce more finished sermons, but they would lack something vital. The best preaching has its roots deep in personal fellowship. The best sermons spring out of contact with men and women and children. There is no message so potent as that which comes from the man well-known, loved, and trusted, by those who listen. A wise old friend delivered the charge to me when I was ordained. He set forth many reasons for being thankful that I was going to be a minister. The one I remember best,—probably because I have so often had cause to prove its truth,—was that after once the people had come to know their own minister, they would rather listen to him than to a better preacher, and would prefer him to the brilliant stranger.

Maltbie Babcock was once asked by some one who felt the power of his prayers how he prepared for public prayer. He answered that his method was very simple. He would look over the congregation, during the early part of the worship, and think about the people; here would be one who had just met a great sorrow; there a man who had met a crisis in business during the past week; here some one who had just entered upon some great joy or satisfaction; here a youth home from school. So his mind would stray over the congregation, and he would be ready to lead them in prayer. Such a method depended on knowing the people through personal contact.

Like those prayers, the best sermons come to a minister out of his relations with people far more than out of his work in the study. That man will preach best who writes and studies in sermon-preparation with a concrete vision of his people before him. That is why one's best sermons cannot be preached to a new set of people without extensive alterations. They are made-to-fit, not ready-made.

So one must be at once preacher and minister.

There is no royal road to take through this tangled

country of pulpit work and pastoral work. The road will twist and turn. But there are certain small suggestions that may have some value.

One's best hope of salvation is through constant and conscientious self-discipline. Here again that much-abused tool, the schedule, is useful. No man who does not plan his time will find time to be both a good preacher and a good pastor. Card-indices, record-books, systematic planning of calls, are all essential to the man who would meet successfully the double opportunity.

Self-discipline is valuable and necessary also in the cutting off of things that do not count. All one's time and strength will scarcely be enough for the work; to let any of it slip away uselessly is to court failure. There is much that is pleasant, that is quite well worth doing, which nevertheless must be cut to small measure, or wholly put away, if a man is to be preacher and pastor. And this applies not only to self-indulgences and personal pleasures, but even more to many tempting opportunities to use time and strength for social and semi-public ends. There are few ministers who can afford to accept invitations to speak which are not fairly in the spirit of their regular service. The best preachers I know will not speak at banquets, or public meetings unless they can give a definitely religious message. They say, "This one thing I do, and this one thing I know,"—not because they are narrow, or bigoted, or over-pious, or fanatical, but simply because they cannot do their proper work if they allow their minds to wander far or frequently from the close vicinity of that work.

If one is wise he will early learn, in rendering service to the community, to accept few or no positions on useless or ornamental committees or public bodies. He will take up the two or three pieces of real public service in which he can work most effectively and most readily, and will cheerfully decline the most pressing invitations to overburden himself. He will especially welcome those openings which offer opportunity for ministry to the personal life of men and women and children in the community. He may well realize also that the best service a minister can render to his community is in giving large place in the life and work of his church to a spirit and program of community service, service of the common good generously rendered without thought of return.

Self-discipline is necessary in the matter of one's ways of working. One must school himself to rapid action; must learn to cut out useless motions and delays of mind and soul; must acquire the ability to turn at once from one interest to another, and back, without cooling down, or losing interest and motion. He must somehow get what owners of motor cars value so highly, the power to "pick up" quickly. One can drill himself in this. I have known many ministers who put several mornings on a single sermon, with great groanings and creakings; and from one-third to two-thirds of the time was absolutely wasted in mooning over the subject; thinking they were thinking; trying to get started instead of starting; beginning with a subject, finding a bit of hard going, and abandoning the path, instead of plunging ahead and going on through. Of course a men may well spend several mornings on one sermon, if he has it to spend, and be only the gainer for it, if he really *works* all the time. One of the best preachers I know tells me he spends five mornings a week on his single sermon. He is so situated that he can. He has no pastoral responsibilities. Happy man! They are great sermons. But that man really works for the whole of the five half-days. He spends no time in unproductive motions.

The man who is, by the grace of God, to be preacher and pastor and administrator in chief in a varied parish, must drill himself to work without waste of motion. He must learn the value of early morning moments, those times so precious, because relatively free from interruption. He must school himself cheerfully to forget one set of duties while caring for another; yet there is one exception to this, for a man may get surprising results if he keeps his prospective sermon floating in his mind, somewhere between the conscious and the subconscious, amid his varied doings through the day and the week.

It is good for a man that he get his theme very early, if possible before the previous Sunday is past. For if it lie in his mind thus for a few days, it will come up with a surprising amount of valuable material gathered out of the corners of his brain.

It helps toward the solution of this double problem if one can get his people to come to him with their specific needs, and not expect him always to seek them. Incidentally it furthers real pastoral work; for one visit from a parishioner, coming on a definite errand, may be worth a dozen calls from the pastor, which may or may not find the parishioner in a mood for serious religious treatment.

Some ministers depend exclusively on the use of office hours, and insist on the right to seclusion except at such specified times. But it is a question if that adequately meets the need. Some of us at least feel the necessity or advisability of greater accessibility.

If personal testimony may be permitted, let me say that for the thirty years of my ministry, I have ordinarily closed my study door only one morning a week, when I prepare my Sunday morning sermon. Even on that morning the door may be opened, and it is understood that it will be opened in case of any need for religious ministry to an individual. All the other mornings the door is open to any one who needs the minister. A reasonable amount of sifting is carried through by a secretary, who tries to eliminate all who come for other than genuinely pastoral help. And if, as sometimes happens, some one enters the study who has the mistaken notion that to sell the minister some insurance or a set of books is business partaking of a spiritual nature, he is quickly made aware of his error. But to the people of the parish, and to all honestly wanting to see a minister on life business, the door stands open. Looking back over rather more than thirty years, I can gladly affirm that, just from the standpoint of the preacher, the policy of the "Open Door" pays richly. Many a sermon has been set back, and some have been ruined, by these personal interruptions. But far more sermons have been warmed, set forward, toned up in their human interest, by live contact with souls; some sermons have sprung, almost full fledged, from unexpected visits of that sort; while some experiences have come out of that policy of the open door, certain interviews and talks, worth more than any sermon, set forever among the precious treasures of one's life.

One must apply self-discipline and unremitting watchfulness to the pastoral side of his work no less than to his preaching. He must save every possible moment of time, must eliminate perfunctory and purely social routine calling, must cultivate an instinct for knowing who really need him, and when.

It is well to realize that, in order to be a good pastor, one need not be ever pursuing his people with social attentions. There is such a thing as over-coddling a congregation. It does the people of a parish a real and considerable service when their minister is able to bring them to see that the demand for attention from the minister is a selfish demand, unworthy of a Christian; that one should join the church "not to be ministered unto, but to minister." When a church member or family takes umbrage at the fact that the pastor has not called for a long time, the minister should call, but not to apologize; rather to show in plain and loving language, and in the name of the Lord, how unworthy of a Christian such an attitude is. The minister who expects from his people a high-minded, self-forgetful generous spirit and attitude will find that attitude growing among them, and will at once lessen the burden of pastoral oversight and encourage his people in the growth of Christian graces. When some one mentions, in a wounded tone, the fact that he has been ill for some weeks and the pastor has not taken notice of the fact, it is rendering a genuine religious service to that person if the pastor, instead of apologizing, plainly asks why he did not let the minister know, thus showing him that he has failed in his duty. It is well to arouse in every possible way in the congregation the sense that the church is a mutual fellowship, in which all care for each, and in which all are eager to lighten the load of pastoral care by earnest coöperation and generous judgment. Such a spirit makes not only an easier pastorate, but a stronger and more Christian church. One of the worst faults of Protestants is the tendency to assume that they have a right to be coddled by their ministers.

The first business of a minister on going to a new field should be to get to know everybody in that field. Following that he should seize every opportunity for real and close contacts with the people at critical moments. An hour, or an afternoon, spent with a man or woman at some time of special need is worth a life time of perfunctory pastoral calling. It is hard to understand the custom into which many ministers of large parishes fall, of limiting their participation at funerals to the service at church or home, declining to go to the grave. All the more in a church where pressure of duties makes pastoral work difficult, should one be eager not to miss the opportunity for sealing personal friendship which comes from revealing oneself as ready to "stand by" in a supreme hour of need. The wise minister will be eager to seize every such special opening for friendly ministry. I have known people to be caught and held in an unbreakable loyalty, which made further pastoral attention practically unnecessary for a lifetime, by a single brief note, coming from the heart, on some sacred anniversary of a birth, a death, a wedding or a confession of faith. It is so easy to keep record of such days, and so easy to make helpful use of them,—if one really loves his people.

There is the heart of the matter. It is still absolutely true that one may speak from the pulpit with the tongues of men and of angels, and bestow all his time and use up his body in pastoral calling, and yet, if he have not love, he is nothing. The first and greatest essential for finding one's way with any real success through the difficult adjustments of preaching and parish work is a great and genuine love for people.

That love will find a way, if only along with it go alertness to seize every possible means of redeeming the time, and conscientious determination to bring to bear every day and every moment a whole self on each part of the task.

There is one more secret, the deepest, of success in this task of finding time and strength to be both preacher and pastor. It is found in one's real faith in God. A man must know how to draw constantly, and very largely, on those spiritual resources which lie in heart-communion with the Unseen. The minister must himself drink deep every day of that fountain of the water of life to which he invites his people. Only a man alive all through can possibly be at once strong in the pulpit, strong in pastoral oversight, and strong in administration of the organized work of a parish. And that life comes out of contacts with God kept fresh and bright. It is not mere pious talk, it is practical sense, that meets us in Luther's dictum, that the busier one is the more careful must he be to maintain his practice of prayer. It is not only beautiful mysticism, it is the best solution of the problem of a busy life, that is found in Brother Lawrence's "Practice of the Presence of God." The priest, Caponsacchi, in "The Ring and the Book," voices a noble and practical ideal for the preacher,

> To have to do with nothing but the true,
> The good, th' eternal, and that not alone
> In the main current of the general life,
> But small experiences of every day,
> Concerns of the particular hearth and home.

To freshen one's soul each morning by quiet, undistracted contact for even a brief moment with the God who meets us in His Word and as we pray; to live through the day, in all its clash of details and duties, in the sense of the presence of the eternal Friend, helps best to make great things stand out, and little things fall into place, and all things take on order and symmetry, as one tries calmly and humbly to do the will of God in Christ.

And what a reward awaits the man who succeeds by God's good grace in being at once a preacher and a pastor. For nothing on earth or in heaven can be more heart-satisfying than the experience of preaching what one knows to be the truth of God, set in strong and worthy words, to people whose hearts are one with the heart of the preacher through long-tested friendliness and fellowship.

CHAPTER VI

IN THE SOCIAL ORDER

THE most obvious and decisive test of the courage and sanity of a preacher is in his dealing with the social and industrial order. It calls for sanity and courage in equal parts. One needs to be not only wise as a serpent and harmless as a dove, but also bold as a lion.

Here is the sensitive point in our modern life. If the preacher is either too timid here, or too rash, he does great harm. The radicals line up on one side and the reactionaries on the other, and the preacher must run the gauntlet. Even if he keeps well in the middle, he will catch a drubbing if he moves forward at all. But woe to him and to the church for which he stands, if he veers to the one side or the other from the course of perfect justice and fairness.

A dozen years ago or more Walter Rauschenbusch told us, in "Christianity and the Social Order," that the really dangerous heresies in the present day are economic rather than theological; that it demands little courage to-day to stand for liberal theological ideas; but that if one would find his way most quickly to the lions, he need only question the accepted economic theories, and industrial methods and practices. It is true testimony. The place of danger to-day is on the front line of the industrial struggle.

It is therefore exceedingly important that the

preacher shall work out with care the problem of his rightful freedom in handling questions related to the social and industrial order. He is bewildered by a babel of voices. On the one hand stand the radicals, who want "to lay the old world low," and "behold the new world rise." Some of them are men and women of deep religious fervor. Many of them are keen-witted enough to discern the tremendous power of religious faith, the potential force that is in the church; and, clearly or dimly, they feel a certain unity of sentiment between the Gospel and all forward moving enterprises. There are few radicals who know Jesus at all, who do not feel His strong attraction.

The papers have recently quoted an alleged utterance of the Russian Soviet government, defending the confiscation of church property. They plead that, inasmuch as the proceeds are to be used for education, they have the sanction of Jesus, who said, "Suffer the little children to come unto me."

From the radical groups in society comes then naturally, inevitably, a strong, passionate surge of protest against what they call the silence of the pulpit, a demand that the church shall champion new economic and industrial theories, or a contemptuous criticism of the church as a defender of the capitalistic order. All this hurts and stings and upsets the preacher. Sometimes it stings him into blind partisanship of radicalism which speedily ends his usefulness in the church. Sometimes it drives him into equally blind reaction which may hold him in his pulpit, but renders him equally useless. Always it makes him uneasy, lest he fail to find the path of real fairness and honor.

Nor is the pressure less from the other side. It is no less impassioned, no less determined, and far more steady. From many influential quarters, whence comes much of the backing of the work of the church, comes a strong and insistent demand that the preachers shall steer clear of social, economic, and political matters, and limit himself and his sermons to the "Gospel." And by the "Gospel" these men and women mean the application of Christianity to the individual soul, and particularly to its preparation for another world. They want the church to be wholly a soul-saving, not at all a life-directing, institution.

Between the two groups the preacher is hard-beset. He honestly wants to do the right thing. How shall he steer his course?

Fundamentally, he must find his guidance where the Master found His. "My judgment is just; because I seek not mine own will, but the will of Him that sent me." Clean hands and a pure heart, a life set on the doing of the will of God, this is the surest and best sort of guidance.

One hesitates to offer counsel, or to attempt to blaze a trail, in so tangled a situation. But certain principles or facts may be asserted with confidence, the clear sight and acceptance of which will at least help toward the finding of the just course.

First of all, in a day like this, when the whole industrial order is under suspicion, when earnest men challenge the very basis of our economic system, no man who preaches should let himself be entangled in any business enterprises, or should draw gain from industrial operations that are open to serious objection. The preacher must be above suspicion.

Aside from any other consideration, the preacher should be like Agassiz, in having "no time to make money." Part of the price one cheerfully pays for the right to preach should be the definite and absolute abandonment of the right to put time or ability into business enterprises. Of course this does not exclude, it rather encourages, thrift; provision for one's family through insurance against death, disability, or accident; and the proper investment of one's savings. But it does mean that one shall not become personally interested in business enterprises; or use his personal fellowships for economic ends; or invest his savings in enterprises of doubtful social value. Too often the influence of ministers has been wrecked on reefs of that sort.

The present industrial order is on trial. Let a minister hold himself fit to sit on the jury.

When the Interchurch Report on the Steel Strike came out, when its serious allegations remained unanswered except by personal attacks on the men responsible for the report, and a single exhibition of special pleading in a sermon widely distributed,—a sermon which did not touch the real merits of the case,—when months went by and the allegations were still unmet, a minister of my acquaintance sold his stock in the Steel Corporation. That was taking the right step to defend his freedom as a preacher. The Report may have been wrong and the Company may have been right; but, in the sensitive state of the public conscience to-day, no preacher can afford to be tied in a profitable relationship with any concern that is under suspicion.

Of course I do not say that every preacher should take the course just described. Every man's conscience must face the matter in the sight of God. Moreover, most of us ministers are fortunately quite free from the necessity of disposing of holdings of any sort of stock. But let us take it as a law from which there is no escape, that he who would be free in the pulpit to discuss the industrial order must shake his hands from the taking of bribes, must see to it that no direct profit comes to him from any questionable operations of the present economic order. There is enough cause for concern over the way we all tend to profit indirectly by the maintenance of the present order with its abuses unchanged.

The preacher who would guard his freedom must also be on watch unrestingly against the insidious danger that the church shall be dominated by money. The church must not be controlled by conservative wealth to its own advantage or in its own interest.

There is a general awakening to the social value of the church for which on the whole we should be deeply thankful. Leading men in the business world are saying good words, appreciative and strong, about the tremendous values of religion, and the consequent importance of the church.

But, while we rejoice in this new appreciation, most of which is absolutely honest and helpful, we need to beware lest there grow up in some quarters an admiration for the church quite like that which one feels toward a good trusty watchdog. When men begin to value the church as a guardian of the present system of things, as a narcotic for social unrest, as giving assurance or help in maintaining present conditions unchanged, it is time to remember the warning of the Master, "Woe unto you when all men speak well of you." It would be a shameful fate for the church of the Living God to come to be valued chiefly as a custodian of property, a defender of things as they are. "Things as they are"—that is Phillips Brooks' definition of the world, to which Christians are not to be conformed.

The preacher may well covet the counsel of men of wealth and of business capacity on business matters connected with the church. Indeed he may well leave such matters largely to their judgment, frankly admitting that his experience in that field is too limited to warrant any interference on his part. But the preacher should set his face like a flint against the current and almost universal tendency to let money talk with authority on any and every subject. Every age has its own peculiar form of idolatry. To-day our danger is "marketolatry," subserviency to the judgment of successful business men, and a tendency to count economic interests paramount. There is a rightful respect due to the man or woman, who, through ability, keenness of mind, daring, or other fine qualities, has amassed a fortune and gained the power that goes with it. But success in business, even the highest success, is absolutely no guarantee at all of wisdom to decide on theological, moral, or religious questions; nor does it argue any superior judgment or wisdom even with regard to economic or industrial principles. Many a man can run a business well judged by financial results, who is wholly incompetent to judge whether the principles on which the business is run are socially just or unjust, morally good or bad.

One of the most serious tendencies in present-day living is the tendency to accept and follow the opinion and judgment of successful men of business rather than of experts in any special line. We educate a man until he has special and expert knowledge on some particular subject. A question arises in that very department of knowledge. And we discount his opin-

ion, on the amazing ground that he is a "professor,"
a student, a man of trained intellect and special knowledge, and take the judgment of a man who, however
successful in the business of making money, may be as
ignorant as a babe on this particular question, his
judgment often being based on nothing sounder than a
childish prejudice.

We must somehow recover the habit of trusting the
scholar in matters of theory, the minister in matters
of religion, the professional man generally in matters
of expert knowledge, instead of deferring to the judgment of the business man on any and every point.
On the *moral* and *religious* issues of industry and social
life the average minister can judge far better than can
the average business man; and the minister must stand
for his superior right and power of judgment in such
matters.

One of the most encouraging and hopeful signs of
vitality in the church is the quick revolt manifested
here and there against unrighteous attempts to bring
or keep the church under the control of financial interests. The whole church is under obligation to the
Young Women's Christian Association for its firm
loyalty to the accepted social creed of the churches,
unmoved by threats of financial loss or even by actual
carrying out of the threats, or by the defection of influential individuals. That great organization never
more worthily than in that course demonstrated the
soundness of its claim to be simply an agent of the
Church of Christ. We owe a real debt to the ministers
of Pittsburgh for the dignified but unmistakably clear
fashion in which they protested against the attempt of
certain commercial interests of that city in the spring
of 1921 to limit the freedom of the church by applying

financial pressure. The preacher must be ready instantly and always to protest against and to repudiate any and every attempt to make the church the servant of property interests, or to influence its policies and pronouncements by allegations of the effect they may have on business, or by application of financial pressure. There is abundant proof in history that the church can far better afford to be poor than to be unjust, or untrue to the highest spiritual and social good of humanity.

The preacher needs to have his eyes open to the fact that, in many cases, men cry out for the "old Gospel," and resist the application from the pulpit of Christian principles and ideals to the social and industrial order, that they plead for an evangel exclusively individual, because they fear the result of applying Christianity to our social affairs. They know that many comfortable conditions in present business would be rudely shaken by a fearless application of the teachings of Christ. They are pleading for an enervated and mutilated Gospel because the real Gospel is distinctly disturbing. They call it the "Old" Gospel, but in truth it is only "Middle-aged." It is not as it came from the soul of the Master, not as it was carried into the world by His apostles. That was a Gospel meant for every fact and phase and part of the life of humanity; its aim was nothing less than to "bring every thought into captivity to the obedience of Christ." Only such a whole, unemasculated Christianity can save this present age, or any other. Let the preacher, on pain of Christ's judgment, stand inflexibly for the right and duty to declare the whole Gospel, in its world-wide application, let it hit where it will and hurt whom it may.

Yet the preacher, if he would be just and right, and fill the place of a true servant of Jesus Christ, must guard himself with equal care on the other side. He must match the emphatic statement that the successful man of business is not qualified by his success to pass judgment on moral and religious questions with as emphatic an admission that the preacher, however good or godly or learned or keen, is not thereby qualified to advise a man how to run his business. There has been far too great a tendency on the part of progressive ministers, alive to social developments, to pass judgment on details, to lay down the law about business method and policy, to tell the business man just how he must act in his business in order to be a Christian. The commercial leader rightly resents such utterances from the pulpit. They are intrusions of the preacher into a realm where he cannot speak with authority. They weaken his influence, rather than strengthen it.

The preacher must not become a partisan. He can successfully and rightly defend himself and his pulpit against attempts to use them in defense of vested rights only by holding himself and his words absolutely clean from the espousal of any particular social propaganda or any special group and its interests. The fatal defect of Professor Rauschenbusch's great book on "Christianity and the Social Order" was the plea at its conclusion that the church definitely line up with the Labor Union Movement. The preacher must jealously guard himself against the slightest rightful suspicion of partisanship.

Here is a task that calls for all the grace that is in a man. It is so easy to be a partisan, so hard to hold the helm straight and sail down the right course. Perhaps one of the best possible proofs that one is keeping straight is that he gets denunciations and criticisms and complaints from both sides. When the radical brands him as a coward, and the reactionary denounces him as a Bolshevist, a preacher may well thank God and take courage. It is like seeing the red and green lights that mark the true course lying in the dark between them.

There are certain simple things the preacher can do to make more sure the finding and keeping of his right and straight course.

Let him be sure that he is well-informed. The apostolic counsel is good here, "Let every man be swift to hear, slow to speak, slow to wrath." Much of the irritation and clashing that has followed discussion from the pulpit of social or economic issues has in reality been caused by hot vaporings boiling off the top of a poorly-informed mind. He who would preach the real Christ to this real age must seize on every opportunity to know the facts of our economic and industrial order. Good books and periodicals are accessible in considerable numbers, which give accurate and valuable information about social principles and industrial conditions. Such volumes as Tawney's "An Acquisitive Society," and the essays on "Social Reconstruction" issued by the War-time Commission of the Federal Council, are indispensable for the preacher who would be well-informed. Even if he sees no way at present to meet or use the facts, let him keep on gathering and studying them. Two men were passing in a railroad car through one of the gigantic industrial districts which lie on the outskirts of our great cities. One of them pulled down the shade. "Why do you do that?" asked the other. "Because I hate to see that dehumanizing place," was the answer. "I know it is wrong, but there is nothing I can seem to do to help it." "There is one thing you can do," came the answer. "What is that?" "Stop pulling down the shade." Face the facts, know all you can of them, read, talk, listen, observe. That is one of the prime requirements for one who would be a good preacher of Christ in an industrial age.

The preacher must be on guard continually against the tendency which is strong in our day to assume, more or less unconsciously, that any book or journal or society or committee which makes statements that reflect seriously on the justice of the present order must of course be partisan and prejudiced. If he is ministering in a church largely made up of men and women who are gainers by the operation of the present economic order, he must quietly but determinedly resist their natural tendency to conclude hastily and as a matter of course that damaging statements, unpleasant revelations, exposures of conditions that call for radical change, must be condemned as untrue. He must stand always for the right and duty to have the light of publicity turned full on every corner of our life, and to face what that light reveals, whoever may have turned it on or however unpleasant or upsetting its revelations may be.

Of course he must be equally on guard against the opposite error, of assuming that the present system of things is wholly wrong, and that any document or committee or group that denounces it must be telling the truth.

Nor must one seek to be well informed by studying only the facts of to-day. He must restudy the Gospel, till he has in his soul the wealth of its social meaning. What is this Gospel in which we say is the hope of man's salvation? It somehow meets every age with a new vision of truth. There is something kaleidoscopic about it. The simple bits of unworldly wisdom thrown together in the New Testament fall into a new pattern of bewildering beauty and freshness, with every turn of the wheel of time. The preacher must get afresh into the heart of the teachings of Jesus and of the apostles, under the guidance of the social spirit of this age. Then he will have something to say. He can speak with authority. There are words hidden away in the Gospels that are bombs for power, arc-lights for radiance. To one who seeks, it seems that the whole New Testament is aglow and alive with a social Gospel. What is needed more than thousands of average ministers, hundreds of Bible classes in average churches, restudying the New Testament to get from it true light on the social application of the Christian Gospel of redemption?

It is of the utmost importance that the preacher should see clearly that it is his business to declare principles and ideals, rather than to make their application specific. I know that that course exposes him to the scornful accusation that he deals only with theory, and never comes to grips with actual facts. It brings out floods of the easy criticism that the pulpit deals only with vague generalities. But nevertheless it is the right course. And he who ceaselessly, week in and week out, sets forth Christian principles and keeps the social ideals of the Gospel shining before the men and women of his congregation, does make a difference, and counts for progress.

Much may be done through forums and meetings of men's and women's associations, to have facts set before the people of the churches, and definite application can thus be made of Christian principles to industrial details. But that should be done by experts. The minister cannot by any possibility become an expert in the details of modern business and industry. By the very conditions of his work he is shut out from authoritative and helpful statement of the application of Christian principles to industrial details.

Let him eschew as dangerous and wrong the impulse to pass judgment on this or that specific application of Christian principle. Let him take as part of the inevitable accompaniment of his position the charge that he deals only in glittering generalities. Let him frankly admit that the Christian business man, and not the preacher, must fit the principles to the particular industrial or commercial situation.

But let him bear hard on the other end of that claim. Let him admit to the Christian business man, every Sunday, that the preacher must be content to proclaim the principles, but let him insist also, every Sunday, that the business man is to put them into operation.

Let there be no uncertain note to the trumpet through which he voices the eternal obligation of the Christian to do the will of God, at any cost, right where he lives and works. Let him clearly declare that any Christian who is connected with a business or industry which is not in full accord with Christian principles has no right to be content, but must either get out of that business, or stay in it to redeem it.

These three things then the preacher may do, and should do, continually, in dealing with the outworking of Christianity through the social and industrial order: First, declare the Christian principles and ideals uncompromisingly; second, point out definitely any and all conditions unmistakably wrong in the light of those principles; and third, insist on the duty of Christian men in business and industry to apply those principles unreservedly, whatever the result. Whenever any bit of the social order is Christianized by this method, the greater glory and credit goes to the business man, who works in the actual. But the preacher does his part, and has his own peculiar satisfaction.

There are two more general convictions or realizations the preacher may well hold constantly in mind as he works his way through the discussion of the social order.

One of them is that he stands in the pulpit a representative of all his congregation. He is not there with a free license to say what pleases him. He has been chosen by a company of men and women, all of them, to say what will be helpful to them in their spiritual life. He must lead, of course. He must not keep his ear too close to the ground. He must have Samuel's ear, not that of Polonius. He is responsible to His Lord and theirs; he must represent the best, most progressive, most forward-moving spirit that is in the people. But always he must speak for all, not for himself alone.

That will inevitably influence the matter, and still more the form, of what he is to say. A very common and harmful mistake made by many a preacher is a half-conscious sense of an invisible audience consisting of all the world, a dulled or even a deadened apprehension of the fact that he is to speak to these particular men and women, and that he must take them as they are and where they are and try to lead them to better thoughts, higher ways, and a deeper and wider practice of essential Christianity. Outside critics help confirm the preacher in this mistaken notion, by judging his words as if they were addressed to all the world, not to a particular set of people. Let the preacher never forget that even the Master of us all, in His last prayer, spoke most of all of what He had done for "His own," those the Father had given Him. The nearer the preacher can keep to the best that is in the heart of all the congregation, the surer will be the effect of his leadership.

The second fact he must not forget is that one great primary function of the church is to hold people of differing groups together. One who has ever come upon Phillips Brooks' conception of the church as a "universal solvent, lying back of all our differences and composing them," can never quite get away from that ideal, is haunted by it always. Sometimes one must preach that which will divide, will arouse opposition. But ordinarily the preacher misses his true opportunity, if he does not choose, so far as righteousness and loyalty to Christ permits, that which will unify the group committed to him, and lead them unitedly into a broader and bigger theory and practice of the Christian life.

Strong men, leaders in the business life of their community, are quite right in feeling and expressing a restless dissatisfaction when a preacher becomes a muckraker, in the currently accepted meaning of that word, an unsparing and unfair critic of present conditions, who rejoices in iniquity as well as in the truth, ever playing up the worst side of social and industrial conditions. But let the business leader remember, and let the preacher help him do it,—that the original idea of a muckraker was different, and far more serious. As John Bunyan drew the man with a muck rake, he was a type not of the carrion crow variety of critic, but of the man whose first and controlling interest is money and material success. It is part of the rightful concern of the preacher not to become a muck-raker in the modern sense of the term; but it is a part of his concern that is immensely more important and serious that he do his best to keep the men and women of his church and of the community from becoming muckrakers in the original sense in which John Bunyan used the word. He will best discharge that function who is not content with criticism and denunciation, or with honest and unsparing presentation of the rightful principles of Christian life and work, but who continually presents a glowing and fascinating constructive ideal of the Christian and his life; who fires men with a vision of the possible meaning and mission of Christianity in the world; who preaches not only a Christ Who steals from door to door, knocking for admission to every heart, but a Christ in the glory of supreme authority over the world, a Christ on the white horse, out to drive the four horsemen back to the pit where they belong, and to make the whole life of mankind godly and brotherly. It is his place to point to the Christ of the Gospel, with His great words and greater spirit of social justice and brotherly love, and proclaim to the whole world of society, of industry, of commerce, of politics, "Neither is there salvation in any other; for there is none other name under heaven, given among men, wherein we must be saved."

It is hard,—one of the hardest things in the world,— to preach the Gospel of the Living God freely in a day of social unrest. It calls for all there is of goodness, wisdom and unselfishness in a man, and then sends

him to the infinite supply of God's grace for that which
will make up his glaring and humiliating deficiencies.
But what an adventure it is, what a life for a man to
live, what a task for a Christian to undertake, what a
joy and glory if he win in it even the least success.
This world of industry will never be right until it is
altogether set on the lines of Christ's clear gospel of
love, brotherhood, service, and faith in human personality. What a privilege to have the right to say
that, to remind men of it, to keep that torch burning
in their sight as they slowly work their way toward
the better day "when the world grows fair."

CHAPTER VII

IN THE WORLD ORDER

MANY years ago a great preacher said, "The world is my parish." But, great man though he was, and deeply as he meant it, he could not say it with one half the truth and emphasis with which the average preacher of our day can make the assertion. For, since his day, the world has become a parish, a neighborhood, bound by bands of steel, and threads of copper, and waves of ether into a vast community of thought and purpose, a world in which each part affects and is affected by every other part.

It is a task at once daunting and inspiring to preach worthily in such an age. How can one stand up and speak in the face of such vast opportunities, in view of so broad a field for the Christian truth and life? How can he handle such a rich confusion of living problems? How can he be free in thought and speech and spirit, in the face of such responsibilities? The Master said long ago, "The field is the world," but what a little world it was! How much more that saying means now! "The field is the world," all this vast, throbbing, varied life to be touched, vivified, unified, redeemed by the Gospel of Christ. "Who is sufficient for these things?" the preacher asks, with an intensity in the question that even Paul could not feel. It is a task calling for courage, poise, insight, breadth and depth of view such as few men possess. No man can rightly fill the place of the preacher to-day who does not always have the world in his view. No parochial or provincial spirit can meet the demands of to-day.

Here emerge some of the most untried and difficult problems the preacher has to face. What are the lines and limits of his freedom? How can he move confidently amid the concerns of the great world-life, with a message big enough to match the age?

Out of the wartime just back of us rises one acute problem, felt more keenly for our realization of failure to face it properly in the sharp exigency which faced us then. What is the right relation of the Christian and of the church to war? And, larger than that, what is the right relation of the church to the state, the organized political life of the nation?

Organized Christianity made a sorry show of itself in its dealing with those questions during the war. It seemed to have no sure mind, no clear voice. It was belabored and denounced on the one hand because it supported and encouraged the war, and on the other hand because it sat like Peter by the fire warming himself, and shirking the responsibility. It is not to be wondered at if, in the eyes of the world, Christ was divided. Some preached non-resistance in His name, and some preached killing enemies in His name. Some individual preachers swung from the one extreme to the other with startling thoroughness and rapidity when our nation entered the war. On the whole the church, here as in other countries, backed the government, once the war was on.

The confusion lingers. One still comes upon lamentations over the failure of the church as shown in its supine abandonment of Christ's doctrine of non-resistance, eloquent pleas to Christians to take the position

that war is in itself and always evil and utterly inconsistent with Christianity; and occasionally also one
finds severe strictures upon the church for its failure
to support more promptly the cause of the right.   Is
it, as a leading American churchman said during the
wartime, the highest function of the church to foster
patriotism?   Or should the church try to set in the
place of patriotism a devotion to humanity, an international mind, proclaiming, as a church in New York
City proclaims, "We know no nation"?

The fact is, the church is as much at sea in this
matter to-day as it was a generation ago about the
relation of Christianity to social and industrial life.
Through the confused issues of that question the mind
of Christ is slowly beginning to take on shape, for those
who really want to see it.   But many years of discussion, with clashing of varied views, and much confusion
and bitterness, had to be passed through before the
question cleared at all.   We must not expect a quick
consensus of Christian judgment on this intricate question of internationalism, of the relation of Christianity
to war and to patriotism.

But this one fact is as clear as the sun at noon of
a cloudless day, that it is high time to awake out of
sleep, and to stay awake; time for the church as a
whole and in all its parts to wrestle with this question
until we know what the mind of the Lord is.   Surely
we can see this at least, that the question of the right
relation of Christianity to war cannot be faced and
decided when war is on.   Then passion rages, patriotism is at white heat; criticism is ruled out; the lid is
clamped down.   Now, after the war, with its hateful-
ness and filthiness still vivid, with a chance for free
discussion and the formation of calm judgment, now

is the time for beginning the long, hard journey that
shall end in clear views and decided convictions, which
may hold as principles of action if ever, as God grant
we never must, we face again the outbreak of a war
in which our country takes a part. The best thought
of the church, and of every man in it, should be given
to the effort to discover what Jesus really teaches and
shows as to the rightful attitude toward war. And,
as we learn better the truth as it is in Jesus, we should
teach it from the pulpits, in our church schools, to all
Christian people. This work should begin now, and
continue uninterruptedly, until the church as a whole
is ready to stand for the real program of Christ. We
hope and pray with all our souls that never again may
war come. But along with that prayer goes another:
that if, in the providence of God, or through the sin-
fulness and stupidity of man, another war should come,
the church may face the emergency with clear vision
and resolute will, knowing what Christ wants, and
ready to do it, whatever the cost. Should the church
take its stand uncompromisingly on the position that
loyalty to Christ demands abstention from war under
any and all conditions? Perhaps not; but let us at
any rate face the question honestly and squarely. The
pacifist at least presents a consistent policy, and bases
it on words and ideals of Christ. He must be met not
by denunciation or evasion, but by clear, patient, unquestionable exposition of the Christian position. To
brand him as a coward, to dismiss him as an unprac-
tical idealist, does not meet the case. The only question is, *What should Christians do?* On the surface,
the pacifist has a good case. He must be met, not by
moving off the ground of Christian ideals, but by going
deeper into that ground to find hid treasure of truth.

It will be richly worth while for the church to set its best thought at this difficult question. Some of us are of the opinion that the pacifist takes the short cut in one of those cases where the longest way round is the shortest way home; that he slashes through a knot which God means us patiently to untangle; that there is need not only of seizing an ideal, but also of keeping touch with common processes of slowly advancing social life. It is Christian to revolt from the hideous cruelties and inhumanities of war; but may there not be something Christian in the refusal to break away from one's fellows if and when this grisly, gruesome, hideous horror of war comes upon that community which we call the nation? "War is hell"; is it not possible that one may at times keep nearer to Christ by descending into hell? The church must so think and speak and act as to parry the keen thrust that she ever condemns war in the abstract, and always supports wars in particular. She must also avoid the Tolstoyan error of turning her back on society and washing her hands of its troubles, saving her own soul.

Moreover there is this which the church may and should do,—see that the case against war is not allowed to degenerate into a cool presentation of economic arguments and considerations. The true accusation against war is not that it wastes treasure, inexcusable as that waste is; not even that it wastes human lives, horrible and tragic as is that ruthless destruction of the world's supreme treasure. The worst indictment against war is found in what it does to the spirits of men, its denial of the principles of Jesus and of all godly and human life and faith. The worst thing is not the hurt that follows the bayonet thrust, but the cultivated hate that delivers it; not the taking of life, but the degradation of the soul and the society of man. The church should be glad of all the help economists can give in freeing the race from the curse of war; but the church should never abandon leadership in the crusade. Something is wrong, fatally wrong, if the church is not ever striding on ahead of every other human institution or group or influence toward a world free from war.

No one sees the true and straight way through that jungle as yet. But it must be found, and it can be found, if the church sets its mind, its prayers, its soul, at the task. Amid all the divided counsels, two things are absolutely clear. One is that we should unitedly, fervently, with ruthless honesty, seek to know the real mind of Christ as to the right of Christians to participate in war; the other is that now is the time to set forth strongly, unremittingly, in season and out of season, the beastliness, the utter abominableness of war, its hideous inconsistency with the spirit and way of Christ; to protest against the idea that war is necessary, natural, or inevitable, and to teach that it is unnecessary, and that to begin it or allow it to come on is a sin of the first magnitude. Every time any one speaks well of war, glorifies it or palliates it, the church should spring forward to strip the golden mask of glory from it and show the hideous beastliness of it. The church should never let a good word be said for war, an excuse offered, an argument advanced in its favor, without protesting in the name of Christ. We should make much of the fact that our own government has plainly and officially indorsed the view that preparation for war makes for war, not for peace. All this we should begin to do now, and this we should carry on unremittingly, until the straight path of the

Lord lies plain before us, and we can go on our way without hesitation or apology or division of counsel. Let every preacher of Christ claim and exercise his freedom to discuss this question of the rightfulness of war with an eye single to the interests of the Kingdom of God, and with frank and utter disregard of any and all other considerations or interests.

Closely allied to this question is another, which arose out of the smoke and tumult of the war, and has lingered on to vex us.

How far is the church bound to support the national government and its policies, and how far is it free to criticize or oppose them? Is it the highest function of the church to foster patriotism? And does that mean that the church and its pulpit must always uphold the existing political order of things?

The exigencies of wartime made necessary a considerable exercise of repression of free speech; it also accustomed us to the ways of propaganda. It would be strange if it had not affected, and that for some time to come, the ability to think and speak freely on matters of critical moment. The preacher needs a steady hand on the tiller and a good eye for signals, if he is to steer straight. There is a large and influential group which thinks it a sufficient statement of the proper attitude of the church to take in a narrow and literalistic way Paul's statement, "The powers that be are ordained of God." There is also a group of radicals which is ever ready to assume that the powers that be must necessarily be wrong.

Straight and concerted thinking is needed to make clear the relation between the church and the state. We are all loyal to the fixed policy of America, the separation of church and state. But we see, with increasing clearness, that the church has a rightful function of moral influence in the life of the nation, and that the nation has a right to expect a measure of support from the church. What are the proper bounds?

In the excitement of the wartime, laws were passed by the Federal Government, and in some of the states, and machinery of espionage and social judgment was set up, which opened the way for unjust and unwarranted intrusion into the separate realm of the church. Attempts were made, some of them able and persistent, to use these laws and agencies as means of compelling churches to support the existing economic order, or of limiting the free use of churches for the expression of public opinion on public questions. It is the unquestionable duty of the church to protest against such policies and acts as are thoroughly opposed to the American policy of a free church in a free state. To insist that patriotism involves the indorsement of any particular social or economic order, and to brand as treasonable or seditious free discussion of suggested changes even of a radical sort, is in itself subversive of the right principles of Americanism.

The church should stand for patriotism. It should be eager to teach its children the principles and ideals of our American political order. It should make much of the great days in the national calendar. Prayer for the nation and for its officers should form a recognized part of public worship. It is a good sign, a real gain, that in many churches the flag, set up in the enthusiasm of the wartime, remains as a symbol of the holiness of the patriotic spirit. There is absolutely no reason why the flag should be displayed in a church in wartime, and not in time of peace. The relation

of the church to the nation must be a constant, not
an intermittent, affair.

But there is need of hard, straight thinking to "mark
the metes and bounds of liberty" in this matter of the
relation of the public utterances of the pulpit to the
national life. The church must learn how to develop
and encourage patriotism without repressing that free
and independent criticism, without which patriotism
becomes a fetich, dangerous to the nation, and menac-
ing to the world. It is one of the conditions of health
in a democratic state that there be in it a free and
independent church, with an influence that can be felt,
loyal to the great inherited principles and ideals of
the nation, standing always for the supremacy of law,
slow to speak on questionable issues, a unifying rather
than a partisan force, but alert to discern and voice
the moral issues involved in public policies, and quick
to resent and protest against any attempt to limit its
right of moral judgment. Every preacher in America
should help work out this unsolved problem of the
proper relation of the church to the nation by practical experiments that shall be at once wise and daring; and by encouraging the holding of conferences at
which the problem may be seriously discussed.

But the function of the church and of the preacher
cannot be limited to protest. Christianity is always
constructive. The Master we follow is one "in whom
is the yea." True Christianity is never satisfied with
attacking an evil; it seeks to set in its place a positive
value.

It would be but a half gain if the church should
work out a clear and consistent policy about participation in war, or even about the broader question of freedom from state control. The church should be at work

at the same time on constructive propositions for making itself a force in the ongoing and upbuilding of a right world-order. There are three lines along which the church, and every preacher in it, should be moving now and constantly; the awakening of an international conscience; the encouraging of coöperation between the church forces of the various nations; and the setting forward of the world-program of Christianity.

We have heard much of late about the need of "the international mind." The need has been shown to be serious by repeated demonstration of the incapacity of the representatives of the people in our national Senate to act in a large way on world-problems. A crude and ignorant nationalism has revealed itself as one of the marked characteristics of American life.

In the work of substituting for this temper an international mind, other agencies than the church may have an even larger part to play. Universities and colleges, Chambers of Commerce, and many other voluntary organizations, may well take the lead. But there is needed not only an international mind, but an international conscience; and here the Christian church finds its opportunity. We should begin to apply to the nation in its international relationships those great principles which are generally accepted as the rightful law for the individual:—"No one liveth to himself"; "we are members one of another"; "bear ye one another's burdens." We must cultivate the sense of universal brotherhood which is one of the essentials of the Christian faith. There is too much of a sense of duty bounded by the Atlantic and Pacific oceans, Canada and Mexico. The conscience of America should be so sensitive to considerations of national honor and international responsibility that it would rise in overwhelming demonstrations when timid leaders of public life play safe in the face of great world-needs and calls.

The preacher who in these days allows himself to remain unintelligent and uninformed about world conditions and the moral aspect of international questions, is unworthy of a place in the pulpit. He should know, and should make known to his people, the facts about the League of Nations, the World Court, the treaties resulting from the Washington Conference, the problems of America's relation to the Far East. He should keep informed as to the changing conditions in Europe and Asia. And he should count it one of the priceless privileges and solemn responsibilities of the pulpit to create or quicken, by ceaseless care, by reiterated word, by ever-present consciousness of its vital and present importance, an international moral sense on the part of the people over whom the Spirit of God has set him.

It is cause for profound satisfaction that, on the whole, the religious forces of America are leading in this work of fostering and expressing a true international spirit. Had the decision rested with the church people of this country, there is scarcely a shadow of doubt that we would now be playing our full part in the League of Nations. When, a year ago, the plan of calling a conference of nations on disarmament hung in the balance, signatures of twenty thousand ministers were secured in less than two weeks to a petition urging that such a conference be called. A similar petition was sent to the Senate this spring, praying for the prompt ratification of the treaties resulting from the Washington Conference. The churches of America are comparatively well organized for the exerting of moral influence in the field of international relations. There are strong and reliable coöperative movements ready to inform, to encourage, to unite forces. Every preacher should be eager to make of his pulpit the strongest possible instrument for the cultivation of an international conscience, and for its free and strong and consistent expression.

The second item in a constructive program for the preacher is that he enter heartily into efforts to bring about the largest possible measure of coöperation of religious forces for the promotion of international good will and friendship.

The church of Christ has an immense and indispensable part to play in the establishment of a true international order. For such an order, however well-drawn and well-started, will fail unless in every nation there is a large force of good will, operating constantly and powerfully. As long ago as 1795, in his great essay on Permanent Peace, Kant laid down as one of the three conditions of lasting peace a large increase of the spirit of good will between nations.

What is there more clearly indicated as the proper province and function of the church, in any and every place, than to take the lead in the great and vital task of providing this universal stock of good will? Here also promising beginnings have been made. Under the very shadow of the war, in the year and month when the storm broke, at a meeting held in the very country where it started, a movement was begun as unpretentious as a grain of mustard seed, but with large promise of growth and use. It is known as the World Alliance for Promoting International Friendship through the Churches. It has councils now in 27 countries. It has a single and simple aim,—to stimulate the church forces in every nation, just as and where they are, without waiting for church unity or any other condition, to begin to act as the natural agents for producing and fostering good will on the part of that nation toward other peoples. Here is something concrete, definite, immediate, and vital.

Every preacher should have a part in this movement; not necessarily in the organization; that is but the servant of the idea and spirit that is so greatly needed, and lies so close at hand. There is no reason why every church in this land, and in every other land, should not be now and always a potent center for good will, where wholesome and kindly feelings shall be encouraged toward the men and women of other lands; where evil rumors and insidious or malicious propaganda shall be faced and shamed back to their unclean holes; whence shall stream forth a steady current of generous good will and confidence and eager readiness to believe the best, that shall form part of the river of life in the midst of the street of the city of God, a river on the banks of which may spring up those trees the leaves of which are for the healing of the nations. There are tasks in the presence of which the church stands abashed, sadly confessing its impotence to act because of its divisions or some other evil condition from which it sees no present way of escape. But here is something the world needs, which the church can begin to give now, this moment, if every pulpit becomes a fountain of international good will and generous judgment. How eager we were in the wartime to play up the good points of the nations that were associated with us in the struggle! How we gloried in the heroism of France, the unyielding independence of Belgium, the dogged courage of Britain, and all the rest! Was it all talk, propaganda? It is the high privilege of the church always to talk thus of our neighbors in the best terms, to set them in the best light, to dwell on that which is finest and highest in their spirit and conduct. It is there now, as it was in the days of the war. Let the church set itself and all its forces at discovering and making the most of the best that can be said for our neighbors. Let it eagerly seize and use to the full every opportunity for bringing together the churchmen of the various nations, that they may know one another better, and be the better able to serve as friendly intepreters of one nation to another.

But the greatest constructive service the preacher can render to the world order is through exalting the world program of Christianity. It is not enough to protest against war. We must set over against the vanishing glory of war the growing glory of the Christian mission.

No preacher is making real use of his freedom to-day who does not enter his pulpit every Sunday with the world in his heart. To be parochial or provincial is to be foredoomed to failure. No church service is right and worthy from which the people do not go away with a wider horizon, and with a deep sense of the bigness of the Christian task. To be true to his calling the preacher must ever feel his religion to be a faith with a mission, and that mission as wide as the world.

The preacher who would make of himself and his pulpit the best possible instrument for true internationalism has right at hand a natural and powerful means. More than ever before, it is a time for lifting up the world-mission of Christianity as the great distinctive fact in the life of the church. The church is a body with a history, a noble history, in which we may well take pride. The church is a body with a creed, a splendid creed which we may well defend. But the church is also a body with a *mission*, and that is its truest glory. Without that mission the history is dead, and the creed vain. Christianity looks forward. The last book in its sacred Scriptures looks forward, not back, catches the glory of the future, not of the past. The Bible ends not in a lock and bolt, but in an open door.

The preacher of to-day will be surest of filling his true place, exerting his full influence, making the best use of his freedom, by exalting the world-mission of Christianity. This is the real case against war; not that it is condemned by abstract considerations; but that it is the antithesis of what the church stands for and is doing; that we have something glorious at which we are aiming, of which war is the brutal and bestial denial.

Here is internationalism at its purest and best, in this missionary movement of the Christian church, which holds the best it has in trust for all men, irrespective of race, color, or tongue; which sends its best to the lowliest, and shows its faith in human brotherhood by freely giving its best for all the world. Can any one doubt that the chief reason why the church forces of this country are so far ahead of average sentiment in the possession of a truly international mind and conscience is that the work of the church in foreign lands has fostered in the church a spirit naturally responsive to international considerations, a readiness to take world views, a real acceptance of Christ's spirit of universal brotherhood?

There is deep and serious need just now for defending the full liberty of the missionary enterprise. In many, if not in all, of the branches of the Church of Christ, a determined effort is being made to shut out from the missionary ranks all who hold modern views of religious truth, to disparage and prevent union movements, and to stand uncompromisingly for some narrow sectarian conception of truth and program of effort. Evil as is the effect of such divisive and reactionary movements here in the homeland, it is tenfold more serious on the foreign field. Two great facts are as clear and sure as sunlight; one is that the best and most influential elements in the Oriental nations will not, and cannot, adopt any religion which cannot live on terms of mutual respect with modern thinking; the other is that Christianity is the only religion that has demonstrated its ability to adapt itself to the modern mind. Those facts put upon the Christians who stand for large freedom, and for the right and duty of the Christian Church to go forward, unafraid, into all the truth, the double responsibility of pushing the enterprise of foreign missions with all their might, and of defending the large and full freedom of that enterprise. For the sake of Christ and of the saving of the world we must keep the dead hand off from the forward movements of Christianity. We must send out the saving Gospel of Christ in terms that appeal to the mind of to-day, with an unfaltering confidence in Him Who said, and still says to the whole race of men, "Ye shall know the truth and the truth shall make you free."

Through the whole range of his thought and activity, the preacher must stand for the things that unite, and against the things that divide; he must stand for comprehensive, not for sectarian, policies and pro-

grams. He must love the world more than any part
of the world, and the truth better than any part of
the truth, and must have an unbounded confidence
in the almighty power of the free spirit of Christ, when
given its way among men.

The world is suffering to-day,—sometimes we fear
that it is dying, for lack of unity, need of something
to hold together its severed and clashing parts.
Matthew Arnold's words come to us as if written for
this very day, rather than for a half century ago:—

> See! In the rocks of the world
> Marches the host of mankind,
> A feeble, wavering line.
> Where are they tending?—A god
> Marshall'd them, gave them their goal.
> Ah, but the way is so long!
> Years they have been in the wild!
> Sore thirst plagues them, the rocks,
> Rising all round, overawe;
> Factions divide them, their host
> Threatens to break, to dissolve.
> —Ah, keep, keep them combined!
> Else, of the myriads who fill
> That army, not one shall arrive;
> Sole they shall stray; in the rocks
> Stagger for ever in vain,
> Die one by one in the waste.

And the true preacher to-day is he who so lives, so
speaks, so looks out upon the world with the eyes and
in the spirit of Christ, that the noble words may be
truly said of him,

> Then, in such hour of need
> Of your fainting, dispirited race,
> Ye, like angels, appear,
> Radiant with ardor divine!
> Beacons of hope, ye appear!

Languor is not in your heart,
Weakness is not in your word,
Weariness not on your brow.
Ye alight in our van! at your voice,
Panic, despair, flee away.
Ye move through the ranks, recall
The stragglers, refresh the outworn,
Praise, re-inspire the brave!
Order, courage, return.
Eyes rekindling and prayers
Follow your steps as ye go.
Ye fill up the gaps in our files,
Strengthen the wavering line,
Stablish, continue our march,
On, to the bound of the waste,
On, to the City of God.

The international function of the Christian Church
was never more beautifully or impressively expressed
than in words that come from an unknown writer in
the second century of our era:

"What the soul is in the body, that are Christians
in the world; for the soul holds the body together;
and Christians hold the world together. This illus-
trious position has been assigned them of God, which
it were unlawful for them ever to forsake."

Here is the opportunity of the Christian Church.
Here is an open door for the Christian minister. He
is the representative of a Leader who made it His
chief function to break down middle walls of partition
and produce one new man; so making peace. He is
servant in the earliest movement in history which has
been international in spirit from the beginning, which
broke through all the artificial restrictions of race, and
language, and aimed at a universal brotherhood, a
movement which has its eye set on the goal of a city
of God in which a multitude from every nation and

people and tribe and tongue shall live together in joy and peace. How can he be anything else than a tireless, impassioned, loyal apostle of world-brotherhood? He will think of his own country as the great unknown prophet thought of Israel, with deep and fervent patriotism, but with the sense that the noblest destiny for his country is that it may heed the call "Thou are my servant. It is too light a thing that thou shouldst care for thine own people. I will set thee for a light to the nations, to be my salvation unto the ends of the earth." His church, whether little or great, his pulpit, whether well-known or humble, will be glorified by the splendor of a mission as broad as the world, and a spirit as high as that of Christ. In the world-order,—yes, in the world disorder of our time, the preacher of Christ will stand not afraid, or abashed, or constrained; but bold, sure, and free in his consciousness of a message and a power that can redeem the world, and that gives to that local church and its pulpit a vital connection with the uttermost parts of the earth. The field is still the world, and the world is still our parish; yes, in a more immediately promising sense than for that man of God, John Wesley, or even for the Son of God, Jesus Christ our Lord, Who has brought us to this place of wider privilege and greater opportunity, that we might bring nearer the Kingdom of God.

CHAPTER VIII

IN CHRIST

OF making many sermons there is no end; and there are libraries of the works of gifted preachers which ministers may use with much profit. But there is one sermon by a layman, a thin volume of some twenty small pages, which no minister can afford to neglect. In that "Christmas Sermon" Robert Louis Stevenson, after describing in his winsome way the sort of man one wants to be, exclaims: "Here is a task for all that a man has of fortitude and delicacy." Such is the judgment of the preacher as he surveys his own particular task. And the longer the time he is privileged to spend in this service the more do its possibilities and ideals loom high above his poor performance. He goes on with Stevenson to say: "He has an ambitious soul who would ask more; he has a hopeful spirit who should look in such an enterprise to be successful." Is it not the preacher of whom this keen and kindly critic is thinking, when he says: "Year after year, he must thumb the hardly varying record of his own weakness and folly. When the time comes that he should go, there need be few illusions about himself. *Here lies one who meant well, tried a little, failed much:*—surely that may be his epitaph, of which he need not be ashamed. There, out of the glorious sun-colored earth, out of the day and the dust and the ecstasy—there goes another Faithful Failure!"

⇒   It is a daunting task, a discouraging career. The minister, more than most men, is haunted his life long by the sense of shortcoming. But how glorious it is to be set at a task which demands that one be at his best every moment, and that in every part of his nature, to be placed by a divine call where the utmost one can be and do will scarce avail to meet the incessant demands. Such a life is life indeed. One wonders that the spirit of generous youth does not leap forward and seize such an opportunity; he wonders why it is that the ministry does not suffer violence, and all college graduates press into it. Perhaps they would, did the church let them see it as it is, unbelittled by traditional and conventional ideas.

We have been thinking of the problem of the preacher's freedom, how he may win and maintain his rightful liberty amid the countless influences that seek to bind him, and hold his soul in servitude. There are two final words to be spoken, in which, far more than in all the rest, lies the secret of the preacher's true liberty. He can be a free man, amid all the conventionalities of his position, and its details of administration; he can walk with easy stride despite the clinging garments of inherited faith and traditional conduct; he can speak freely on critical and controversial themes; and in it all maintain himself and his influence in strength and usefulness, if he has found two great and simple possessions, which are in truth one and the same; they are freedom from self, and freedom in Christ.

Freedom from self; that is the preacher's first, and last, and deepest need. Given that, he is free indeed. The dark shade that hovers over his best work is his own shadow. He never finds himself until he has lost himself. He is never free until that old man of the sea is off his back. And how he clings! How he finds his way back, and springs on one's shoulders, and holds tight, just when one thinks he is free forever from the incubus!

A strange tale is that little story from the Norse-land of a man who was uneasily though dimly aware of some one e'' following him. He could not be sure that he heard ... ps; he could see no one; but the consciousness of a malicious sprite or troll dogging his steps grew ever clearer. He wandered far to escape the pursuer, even to the lonely, frozen North; but the steps sounded ever louder. At last he turned suddenly,—and was face to face with himself.

That is the demon that dogs the steps of the preacher, holding him back from the truest success, making him fearful when he should be free. Somehow he must be saved from himself.

It is not only nor chiefly in its coarser forms that self-interest hurts and hampers the work of the preacher. We may leave aside these more obvious and outward aspects of the self-centered life. It is axiomatic that a minister can do nothing but fail, if self-advantage bulks large among his motives. What we have in mind is the subtler play of the self-motive.

Why is it that the preacher cannot speak with freedom? Most of all because he cannot get free from himself. We have a way of saying, when a speaker rises to a height of true eloquence, "He forgot himself in his cause." There is the true freedom. "He that hath ceased from his own works, doth enter into rest." I never hear Kreisler play that I do not say to myself, "There it is! That is what the preacher longs to be, and should be, a man who has forgotten self, and become a perfect instrument for the use of the master whose thought he is expressing."

That which strikes one about the greatest preachers is their self-unconsciousness. But we are mightily mistaken when we suppose that this is in every case a native gift, or an easily acquired attitude. It may be the supreme and most hardly won achievement of their souls.

Patience, discipline, hard work, practice,—these are absolute essentials, without which no man can preach effectively. But these alone can never carry him to any real success as a spokesman for God. If he works by clockwork his hearers will see or hear the wheels go round. The wheels must be there; but the spirit of the living creature must lift up the whole in a daring flight of self-forgetfulness.

The problem of the preacher is not unlike that of the devotee of a sport which has great charm for ministers. One cannot become a good golfer without hard work, steady practice, careful discipline and drill. But woe to the man, who, when the game is on, goes into it with the spirit of patient, plodding attention to detail; who is carefully conscious of himself each moment, watching every movement of wrist and arm and foot with painstaking devotion. The works of the flesh must be lost in the life of the spirit, or he will never enter into the joy of the game.

So the freedom of the preacher must be above all freedom from himself. Not only self-indulgence, but self-pity, self-excuse, self-contentment, all the seven devils of self-concern must be exorcised, if one is to play freely, gladly, and helpfully the great part of a preacher for God to men.

Of course, this is but one way of stating the problem. One might say, with equal truth, that what the preacher really needs is, out from among the many possible selves that lurk within him, to choose, to develop, and to bring to dominance his best and highest self. But it is no less true, and more vivid, to picture the task as that of winning freedom from oneself.

This is what the preacher needs, not only in the delivery of his message, but to conserve his strength and insure his value, in the details of his ministry to men and women.

Nothing so clears the mind of doubt, and sets the path of duty in a shining light, as does the possession of a soul clean from self-concern. Those close decisions which wear men's souls, between conflicting lines of duty and of opportunity,—and ministers have more of them to make than most men,—are amazingly forwarded when one's soul is utterly free from fear of consequences to oneself, absolutely careless as to the personal outworking of the decision. Nothing so unfits one to give helpful counsel to souls in difficult personal problems as the intrusion of self-concern. Better close one's study door, and turn away the troubled seeker after counsel and sympathy, than admit him to the presence of a mind only half-attentive, the keener half restless to get back to the unfinished and interrupted task. He only is free whose soul is whole at each moment and for each varying opportunity; and the secret of that freedom is freedom from self-love and self-concern.

Nor does the problem stop with the matter of freedom from one's personal and petty concerns. There is a larger self from which one must be set and kept free. Each of us is closely connected with the group-life;

he belongs to a social circle, to a particular denomination of Christians, to a nation. It is terribly easy to have one's loyalty to these group-interests become a mere enlarged self-interest, so that one's denominational loyalty, or one's patriotism, shall be nothing more nor less than a more diffused, less offensive, but no less dangerous egotism. The jingo in politics, the bigot in religion; these are but cases of enlarged selfishness.

How can one escape from this haunting, harmful presence of himself, so that, in his message, and in his ministry, he may serve with perfect freedom and joy, set at liberty from the ball and chain of his own self-consciousness and self-interest?

This is but one phase of the great human, religious problem for the solution of which the preacher is sent of God into the pulpit and into the ministry. Here is our answer:—the preacher must experience in his own soul, and throughout his life and work, that salvation which he offers from God and in the name of Christ to all men who hear him.

Through all the shifting confusion of present-day thinking on religion one can discern a question that means more than any other: What is salvation? What is it really that we offer men in Christ? The lack of a clear and definite answer is the weakest element in the message and ministry of the church to-day. The eschatological answer is no longer convincing. Men are more or less indifferent to a religion that offers them nothing more immediate than the issue between heaven and hell. Religion must make a vital difference now. The answer in terms of character is vague and cold. It seems to have more kinship with Marcus Aurelius than with Jesus of Nazareth. Are we not coming to see with increasing clearness every year, that the essence of salvation is being set free from oneself? The man most truly saved is he who has entered most fully into the experience of forgetting himself in a great adventure, a compelling loyalty, so noble, so glorious, so hard, yet so hopeful, that his whole soul is claimed by it, leaving no shreds of himself to be caught at and held and distracted by the motive of self-interest.

It is in such terms that Jesus Himself presented salvation, and called men to come and secure it. His is never the cry of "safety first." "Come and be saved" never means "Come and be preserved"; it always means "Come and be spent," in that earliest and purest Gospel of Jesus' own words and thoughts. He came to men lost in themselves to save them from themselves. So far as one can venture to put the experience of Christian salvation in a phrase, we may say that it consists in *the joy of self-forgetfulness.*

Here we come upon the kernel of truth in a fantastic and repulsive dogma which held sway in New England theology a few generations ago. It was held that no one is truly saved unless and until he is willing to be damned if that be to the glory of God. It was a monstrous heresy, and we give thanks to the Spirit of Light that its shadow has been driven out. Yet somewhere within every doctrine that has gripped the souls of men is a truth; and the truth below that monstrous dogma is this great fact that no one is truly and fully and really saved who has not ceased to care very much about himself; who cannot say with a whole heart, "God be glorified, no matter what happens to me"; who has not really lost interest in the petty question of his own fortune, or success, or even that enlarged self of the group to which he belongs, because with all his heart and soul and mind and strength he is in love with something greater and worthier.

Thus the preacher's hope of attaining that freedom from self which is the root and basis of all true liberty of prophesying lies altogether in his entering for himself, really, wholesomely, utterly, into that saving grace of God which he offers to all men. He must himself feel and know, as an experience that is at once a vivid joy and a calming and steadying influence, he must know in pulpit and pastorate and personal life, through all his word and work and walk, the grace of God in Christ that saves a man from himself, by captivating his soul with the glory of a cause, a mission, by claiming all his love and loyalty for the person of a divine leader, in all the world the only object worthy of a soul's whole love.

It is "in Christ" that the preacher finds that freedom which is the condition of his true success. The phrase comes from the greatest of Christ's men, the supreme example of the missionary, the churchman, the man of God at the business of saving and serving the world of men. To Paul everything was possible, because everything was "in Christ"; and "if any man be in Christ, he is a new creature; old things are passed away; behold, they are become new"; for this is what it means to be "in Christ"; that one henceforth lives "not unto himself, but unto Him." "The life that I now live in the flesh, I live by faith in the Son of God."

The simplest, surest, straightest way,—I do not hesitate to call it the only way,—to that freedom from self in which is the essence of all liberty is "in Christ."

He has found the way to freedom in preaching who can say, "To me to live is Christ."

To lose oneself, and find oneself, in Christ,—that is the simple but hard solution of the whole problem. It is at once simple and hard because it demands the whole of one; no part can suffice. It is "neck or nothing, heaven's success, or earth's failure."

Here is the condition of freedom, and its assurance, in each of the divers fields through which we have strolled. How shall the youth in whose soul is a prophetic spark keep that precious gift from dying, fan it most surely into a flame ever brighter and clearer? How shall the church escape the shame and condemnation of quenching the prophets in their youth, or stoning them in their maturity; how shall the church be wise enough to cherish and develop to the utmost this best gift of the spirit of prophecy? "In Christ" is the answer. The youth of sensitive soul, who sees visions and hears calls from the unseen, will find at once the fire of his imagination fanned and fed, and his sanity and balance held well-poised, so that he may become neither an echo, nor a discord, but the true voice of the Living God, if he loses himself and finds himself "in Christ"; keeping close to Him, catching His spirit, learning ever more of His wisdom, until he sees with the Master's eyes, feels with His heart, thinks with His mind.

Where lies the real hope that the church shall ever cast off its fears and reactions, loosen its timid hold upon the past, and welcome the spirit of free prophecy as its guide? We talk of enlightenment, and education, and progress, as the necessary conditions; and it is all true; but it is all less than the truth. What is needed, all that is needed, for the attainment of that unity, progress, spirituality, and power which all true sons of the church long to see realized in its life, is that the church should forget everything else "in Christ"; that it should mean what it says when it asserts that "Jesus Christ is the only Head of the church." Why, we have taken that as if it were nothing more than a mere denial that the pope is the head of the church. If once it were taken all through the length and breadth of the church as a denial of the right of any man, any teacher, any creed, any council, Luther, Calvin, Augustine, Paul himself, to supreme authority, the assertion that Christ alone is our Master, so that we care only for that for which He cared, insist on that only on which He insisted, and take Him as our sufficient Lord, the church would leap forward toward that unity and victory for which we have long prayed in vain. For then the church would be free; the prophets would have free course; the word of God would live and glow and burn before men.

It is a sober and saddening fact that the three issues which have most effectually divided Christians into disputing and warring camps in the last half-century, the inerrancy of the Scriptures, the virgin birth of our Lord, and the Apostolic Succession of the ministry, are, each and all, matters on which Christ never said a syllable, to which, so far as we know, He never gave a thought. It ought to make a Christian sick at heart to realize that the table of the Lord, established by Him to be a symbol and means of fellowship, is still a means of separating Christians one from another; and all because we set other commandments alongside of, or ahead of, that which He deemed worthy to be His one commandment. We think we know more than He does.

The church will be free when it is willing to lose itself and find itself wholly "in Christ." Then will come days of prophecy beside which that glorious era, the Eighth Century before Christ, will seem but the faint glimmer of early dawn in contrast with the shining of the sun in his glory.

There is no way by which the preacher may walk more readily and more surely on the straight and narrow path that leads between the extremes of self-indulgence and asceticism in his personal life and habits, no way by which he may be more easily and wholesomely free as a man among men, in the world and yet not of it, at once unmistakably spiritual and wholesomely human, than by living his life "in Christ," so that he is free from the judgments of men, careless of their criticisms, yet never harming a weak soul through the exercise of a selfish liberty. Christ kept to that path; never a soul so free; never a soul so considerate. To catch His spirit, to walk in His way, to know nothing and care for nothing save Jesus Christ, is to have the open secret of a life that shall give force to the words spoken from the pulpit.

Nor is there any other one fact or force that can so surely and steadily give to a man's utterance that freedom for which the preacher always longs, that "liberty" which is the joy of preaching, as can a complete, quiet, joyous trust in Christ. Many a preacher knows what it means to pass through a week in which proper pulpit preparation has been impossible, driven away, crowded out by duties a servant of God could not ignore, to come to the hour of worship utterly unready, to say to himself and to God, "This is no longer my concern; it is God's; He must speak through me, and He will"; and then to find such joy and power in the message as has seldom made itself evident. This is something wholly different from careless, indolent, magical reliance on Divine inspiration as a substitute for hard work and careful thinking and self-discipline. It is only in the preacher's extremity that God's opportunity comes. But to know in one's soul, beyond all question, that God is there, and may be trusted, that He is the ultimate hope and will not fail, that is to find freedom and joy in the pulpit such as comes from no other source. It sets one free from the fear of men, from the dread of failure, from the curse of self-consciousness, from the haunting sense of incapacity. There is a special meaning for the preacher in the great assurance, "They that wait upon the Lord shall renew their strength; they shall mount up with wings as eagles."

It is by dwelling "in Christ" that the preacher can best preserve his serenity of soul, his clearness of vision, his spiritual sensitiveness, while busy with the innumerable details of administrative work and the care of individuals in his parish. It makes a difference which is described adequately only when we call it infinite, when he must turn from his thoughts and study and kindling visions to deal with the needs of some individual visitor, if he sees there only an interruption to be dealt with as patiently as possible, or if he hears the voice of the One he loves best and longs to serve, saying, "Inasmuch as ye do it unto this one of mine, ye do it unto me." When he greets the intruder in that spirit, he goes back to his work and thoughts actually refreshed, entering into the experience of the Master who said, "I have meat to eat that ye know not of," because His soul had been invigorated and refreshed by talking with a poor, foolish, sinful woman who broke in upon His rest when He was weary. It is the man who is really living "in Christ," who best solves the difficult and delicate problem how to be a good pastor and a strong church leader and at the same time maintain the freedom of soul necessary to true success as a preacher.

How can one walk at once easily and steadily, turning neither to the right hand nor to the left from the path of simple truth and honor, in his dealing with the tangled thoughts of present-day theology? How can he lead the men and women into the full light, without blinding and dazzling them? How can he be faithful in meeting the need of youth for brave dealing with truth, and the need of older minds and souls for quiet joy in the religion which has proved their strength? Here, as everywhere, the answer is simply "in Christ." The man who will, at any cost, by any sacrifice, whatever the consequences, uncover whatever of the truth in Christ is hid by current and accepted theology; but who gives little heed to theology old or new which is not an interpretation of Christ and His Gospel; the man who in the pulpit has no time for anything but the truth as it is in Christ Jesus; will be at once free and helpful; a true leader of the souls of men into the greater light, without being a needless disturber of the peace. He will disturb the peace of some souls, because it is an ungodly, an unchristian peace, out of which they need to be shaken. But the preacher who always holds himself and his message "in Christ" will always be free and sound and strong and helpful.

It is by being thoroughly at home "in Christ" that

the preacher will most surely find his way into and
along the true path of sound influence on the social
and industrial outworkings of Christianity. Let him
preach his own views, assert his own authority, stand
for his personal and private convictions, and he will
surely get into trouble, as he ought to expect. But
let him speak always out of a real knowledge of Christ's
principles and ideals, a deepening and growing knowledge of them, and out of a passionate and utter loyalty
to Christ which makes him neither afraid of what
others think, nor solicitous for what he himself thinks,
but desirous only that the way and thoughts and will
of Christ shall have free course, and he will preach
with freedom, without fear, and without disaster, on
this hard and confused matter. He knows, and his
people know, that his business in the pulpit is to make
clear the whole teaching and spirit of the Master as
applied to the whole life of man and his world; and
once they know that the preacher has only the one
desire, to find out what Christ wants and to declare it,
he will be free, and the best of them will defend his
freedom even when it challenges their accepted ideas
and judgments, and cuts across their personal or group
interests.

How shall the preacher be free to range through this
newly opened, vast, uncharted field of international
relations, of world-conditions and world-needs and
world-policies, save as he thinks and speaks always
"in Christ"? It is Christ Who has set in the world a
fellowship of men meant to become a brotherhood of
man. He is the author and the perfecter of true internationalism. The preacher will speak most freely
and most authoritatively about the world-order and

its ideals who speaks in the name and in the spirit of
Christ.

Here is the simple principle, in which is "the conclusion of the whole matter,"—that he who would be
a preacher in the Christian church must himself be
heartily a Christian. The Christian religion, as it has
come down through the ages, has gathered much to
itself, custom, creed, tradition, organization. It has
entered more and more intimately into the life of the
world; it has become a part of the common ongoing
of our communal life. At times the mass of accumu-
lations catches and jams and blocks the flow of the
living water; then men who love pure doctrine and
pure life more than they love their own comfort must
risk much to break up the mass and set the water
flowing again. Often we long to get rid of all the
accretions, good and bad, valuables and rubbish together, and get back to primitive and idyllic purity.
We cannot do it. The slogan "Back to Christ" is a
poor one. What we need is to go on with Christ.
God has put the church in the world, that it may work
out, in and with the life of the world, the perfect and
complex life of the Kingdom of God. But that great
end can be worked out only as men and women are
truly Christians, honestly living and thinking in terms
of Christ and His simple, divine, eternal ideals. The
preacher must be, above all, and below all, himself a
Christian, with the patience of Christ that ever comes
not to destroy but to fulfill, and with the free spirit of
Christ, that will see and say what is the truth of God.
"Where the spirit of the Lord Christ is, 'there is
liberty."

Emerson might have had in mind the preacher and

his life of "freedom inserting itself within necessity and turning it to its profit," when he said, "It is easy in the world to live after the world's opinion; it is easy in solitude to live after one's own; but the great man is he who, in the midst of the crowd, preserves with perfect sweetness the independence of solitude." So Christ lived. And the surest way so to live is to live in Him.

There are other steps that follow us, another figure that haunts us ever, beside that persistent little troll, or demon, that turns out to be oneself. There is the presence Francis Thompson felt, the hurrying steps he heard, the constant call of a "love that will not let us go," the Heavenly Friend ever at hand, in whom we find our perfect peace and freedom. Think of the great preachers of the past. How they have differed, in gifts, in service, in manner, in method, in everything! Yet in one great matter they have been alike. Always the great preacher for Christ has lived and spoken and served and suffered and doubted and triumphed or faithfully failed, "in Christ," in the power of an unreserved, deep, glad, complete loyalty to Jesus Christ, in whose name he has spoken. This is the only way. Yes, Christ can and does take even the "Faithful Failure," the man most conscious of his poor efforts, and transfigure his ministry, even as out of His own cross came the glory of the Resurrection and of man's hope of the Kingdom of God.

Never was the truth about a man and his calling better expressed in a material form than in the memorial statue to Phillips Brooks, where back of the preacher, protecting, strengthening, inspiring him, life of his life, truth of his thought, joy of his spirit, is the figure of Christ. In that unseen presence is to be found the secret of the power and influence felt and seen as the true preacher moves among men.

On all sides one hears voices to-day, strident, insistent, critical, accusatory voices, telling us what is wrong with the church, what it needs, what it must be. We who know the church from within, who love it and serve it, and through it try to serve truly God and man, know well that what the church needs is a new birth of that freedom wherewith the Son makes us free, a fresh surge of the spirit of prophecy, a new assurance in its message, a spirit more at home in the great things of God than in the little thoughts of men. Who shall find and show and make glorious the way of such freedom if not the preacher, the leader of the life and thought of the church? And where shall he find it, if not "in Christ"?

The greatest need of the preacher to-day, needed even more than better preparation, and improved methods, more than any and all other qualifications or possessions, is the free spirit once given shape in noble words by that rarely gifted man of God, Frederick W. Robertson, as the expression of his own ideal:—

"To live by trust in God,—to do and say the right because it is lovely; to dare to gaze on the splendor of naked truth, without putting a false veil before it to terrify children and old women by mystery and vagueness,—to live by love and not by fear; that is the life of a true brave man, who will take Christ and His mind for the truth, instead of the clamor of either the worldly world or the religious world."